D1716325

Jack The Ripper
The Celebrity Suspects

I'm a celebrity, get me out of Whitechapel!
Policeman: 'I'm taking you in for questioning about the 'orrible murders'.
Suspect: 'Don't you know who I am?'

3,95

Jack The Ripper
The Celebrity Suspects

Mike Holgate

The
History
Press

Acknowledgements

The author would like to express his appreciation for access to archive material, books, newspapers and online resources available at the John Pike Local Studies Room, Torquay Central Library.

Illustrations

The illustrations in this book have been obtained from antiquarian books and the following magazines and newspapers: *The Graphic, Illustrated London News, Illustrated Police News, Le Journal Illustré, The Penny Illustrated Paper, People, New York Herald, Punch.*

First published 2008

The History Press Ltd
The Mill, Brimscombe Port
Stroud, Gloucestershire, GL5 2QG
www.thehistorypress.co.uk

ISBN 978 0 7524 4757 5

Typesetting and origination by The History Press Ltd.
Printed in Great Britain

Contents

Throughout the text individuals are cross-referenced in **bold** fonts to indicate that there is more information in a separate chapter dedicated to that person.

Introduction

JACK THE RIPOFF

There are liars, damn liars and people who write books about Jack the Ripper.

ANTIQUARIAN CRIME-BOOK DEALER, JACK HAMMOND

Rippermania has driven a 120-year-old investigation to identify the depraved killer of five prostitutes in the East End of London. A fanatical group of researchers dubbed 'Ripperologists' devote their lives to the quest and continually serve up a never-ending list of compelling and totally fascinating suspects. With well over 200 names already in the frame, there is little chance of Jack the Ripper becoming an endangered species. Publishers playfully invite Scotland Yard to close the file on the case with hopeful subtitles such as 'The Final Solution' or 'The Mystery

The Ripper strikes again!

Jack the Gorilla!

Solved' – although each new revelation ensures that the most credible solution will never be universally accepted. With an insatiable readership to feed, every conceivable angle has been covered to produce 'evidence' against individuals, including desperate attempts to conduct psychic investigations and analyse astrological charts. The current growth in the 'Ripper' market reflects modern society's obsession with 'celebrity' and this book focuses on the many famous personalities whose, admittedly, often rather dubious reputations have been further tarnished by sources eager to accuse public figures of being informants, suspects, accomplices or conspirators implicated in the case of the world's most notorious serial killer. Safe in the knowledge that dead celebrities can't sue – and never allowing the facts to get in the way of a good story – authors have imaginatively named and shamed royal figures, prominent politicians, eminent artists and successful writers. The evidence against each of them is flimsy at best – and, let's face it, they can't all be guilty – although conspiracy theorists would have us believe that the Crown, with cooperation from the government and top police officials, turned a blind eye as a band of secret-society cutthroats committed the atrocities in an effort to either appease Irish nationalists or cover up the sordid love lives of a choice of two princes of the realm.

Gathered within these pages are the Victorian 'A' list contenders for the prestigious title of Jack the Ripper – including one plucked at random from my own imagination. Setting aside my admiration for the glorious proposition that the murders were committed by an escaped gorilla – a marvellous anecdote and refreshing antidote to the human celebrity jungle – I temporarily inhabit the fantasy world of the more unscrupulous Ripper buffs and, with deference to the home of my own publisher, Gloucestershire, conjure up a (tongue-in-cheek) suspect in the gargantuan shape of the county's most famous son, no less a personage than cricket legend W.G. Grace!

Mike Holgate
March 2008

I

Queen Victoria (1819-1901)

A REIGN OF TERROR

And are Queen Victoria's lieges to be scared almost to fits,
And helpless women murdered and cut up in little bits,
Because the eyes of Justice, which proverbial are blind,
Won't open just a little way and help us for to find
The livin', breathin', vampire which on blood enjoys its feast,
As now pervades and poisons the regions of the East?

JUDY, 10 OCTOBER 1888

Queen Victoria celebrated her Golden Jubilee in 1887, marking fifty glorious years when the nation's naval supremacy and military might established the British Empire as the world's leading power. In the wake of the Industrial Revolution the country had also enjoyed unparalleled economic prosperity, which brought about vast social changes to towns and cities. Nowhere was this more evident than in London, which, during the sovereign's long reign, experienced a population explosion, quadrupling in size and creating a squalid, poverty-stricken lower class, living in areas of poor housing where unemployment, crime, drunkenness and prostitution were rife. Charles Booth would publish the findings of his sociological survey *Life and Labours of London* in 1889, by which time, the Establishment had already received a violent indicator about the worst extremes of social evil from someone whose name would become as memorable as the monarch's – the world's first serial sex killer – Jack the Ripper.

Murder in the heart of the city's East End was commonplace, yet, the ferocity of the 'Whitechapel Murders' and the savagery inflicted on the victims immediately attracted lurid headlines in the press and raised awareness of the appalling social conditions. Estimates of how many women were targeted by the killer vary from three to thirty between 1887 and 1891, although the consensus of opinion is that the same hand slaughtered five prostitutes over an

Charles Booth.

eight-week period in Autumn 1888. The first of these 'canonical' victims was struck down on 31 August, when the mutilated body of Mary 'Polly' Nichols was found. Unable to afford a bed in a lodging house, she had been wandering the streets trying to raise money by prostitution when her throat was viciously cut right through to the spinal column before her skirts were raised and her abdomen ripped open exposing her intestines. A week later Annie Chapman met a similar fate, when her intestines were removed and laid neatly on the ground, while her womb was removed and taken away by her killer. On the last day of September, an infamous 'double event' occurred when two women were slain in a single night. Elizabeth Stride was last seen talking to a man 'respectable' in appearance – less than thirty minutes before her body was discovered. This time there was no mutilation and blood was still seeping from the dead woman's throat, indicating that the Ripper had narrowly escaped detection. Forty minutes later, the psychopath struck again when he slashed the throat and stomach of Katherine Eddowes. With maniacal zeal, her throat, face and abdomen were slashed and a kidney and womb removed. The worst atrocity was saved for the final victim Mary Jane Kelly who was attacked in her lodging house on 9 November 1888. When a rent collector called on the streetwalker, he peeped through the window and spotted her naked, bloodied corpse lying on the bed. Her face had been brutalised almost beyond recognition; flesh removed from her abdomen and thighs was found on a bedside table, while the breasts had been sliced off and her heart extracted and removed from the scene of the crime.

Queen Victoria took a special interest in the murder investigation by forwarding her own opinions and suggestions to her ministers. The day after the final murder she advised:

This new most ghastly murder shows the absolute necessity for some very decided action. All these courts must be lit, and our detectives improved. They are not what they should be. You promised, when the first murder took place, to consult with your colleagues about it.

The fact that this innocuous memorandum proposing improved street lighting also refers to the Queen having taken action 'when the first murder took place' has been interpreted as proof that she had some inside knowledge of it being the first of a sequence. In this respect, it has been argued that she had some sinister motive to apprehend the villain whom she knew to be a close member of her own family. Suspicion has fallen on her notorious womanising son the Prince of Wales, or allegedly syphilitic grandson the Duke of Clarence who have both been accused of being Jack the Ripper. Alternatively, it has been suggested that there was a 'cover up' of the amorous activities of either prince. In the case of the **Prince of Wales**, he is said to have had a relationship with the aforementioned Mary Kelly, who became pregnant with his child and a scandal was averted when she and her friends were silenced by two young lawyers, Montague Druitt and **James Kenneth Stephens**. The royal conspiracy theory surrounding the **Duke of Clarence** was supposedly organised by the Prime Minister **Lord Salisbury** with the

Queen Victoria.

cooperation of the Metropolitan Police Commissioner, **Sir Charles Warren**. In this scenario, Queen Victoria's physician-in-ordinary **Sir William Gull** was recruited by the Freemasons to eliminate women attempting to blackmail the government with embarrassing knowledge that the Duke had entered into a secret marriage and fathered the child of a commoner. Aiding and abetting Gull in his grim task was either artist **Walter Sickert**, or head of Scotland Yard CID **Sir Robert Anderson**. Orchestrated by former Chancellor of the Exchequer **Lord Randolph Churchill,** their mission was to eliminate all witnesses and save the monarchy, which was increasingly coming under attack. In 1890, the American *Daily Northwestern* referred to the unsavoury lifestyles of the Prince of Wales and his son the Duke of Clarence and cited them as the worst examples of the 'debauchery which too conspicuously punctures European royalty'. The newspaper blamed their sordid behaviour and the growing threat of revolution on Queen Victoria's family relationship to virtually every head of state on the Continent and her marriage to her Bavarian cousin Prince Albert, a union which had produced nine children: 'The inbred crowd of royal stock of all Europe is becoming sadly deteriorated both bodily and mentally, and cannot long, in any event, survive the strength of a higher order of governmental civilization which the common people are attaining'.

2

The Prince of Wales
(1841-1910)

The Playboy Prince

God will never allow such a wicked man to come to the throne.

A ROYAL FOOTMAN ON THE PRINCE OF WALES

Queen Victoria's eldest son and daughter-in-law, the Prince and Princess of Wales, celebrated their Silver Wedding Anniversary in 1888. Throughout the relationship, the promiscuous prince – christened Albert Edward, though known as 'Bertie' to his friends and 'Dirty Bertie' to his detractors – had enjoyed numerous salacious affairs. The first scandal broke in December 1861 as preparations were being made for his forthcoming engagement to the daughter of the heir to the Danish throne, Princess Alexandra. Rumours of the prince's lustful pursuits at Cambridge University persuaded his parents to send him on a military exercise in a remote part of Ireland. However, the plan backfired disastrously when actress Nellie Clifden boasted of how the prince's friends had smuggled her into the royal army tent and the amorous liaison was soon the talk of London. Upon his return to Cambridge, his furious father Prince Albert, who fell ill during the journey back to Buckingham Palace and succumbed to typhoid fever, berated Bertie about his irresponsible behaviour. As Queen Victoria withdrew from the public eye and went into decades of prolonged mourning, she blamed her son for the loss of her husband and told one of her daughters, 'Much as I pity I never can or shall look at him without a shudder'.

The incidental death of his father seemingly did not trouble the incorrigible prince whose sexual conquests, including famed actresses Lillie Langtry and Sarah Bernhardt and a string of society beauties Daisy Brook, Alice Keppell and Jennie Churchill, continued unabated following his marriage in March 1863. The largely pro-monarchy press, who delighted in pillorying politician **Charles Parnell** and author **Oscar Wilde** for their extra-marital activities, patriotically avoided criticising the heir to the throne who feared no embarrassing revelations even when openly accompanied by his mistresses in public. Whiffs of scandal only circulated

The Prince and Princess of Wales at the time of their marriage in 1863.

when members of his own elite royal social circle broke ranks. In 1869, Bertie was compelled to appear as a witness in the divorce court after being named as one of the many lovers of Lady Mordant. He was able to deny the affair without contradiction when her ladyship was declared unfit to give evidence – suspiciously certified insane and institutionalised at the behest of her husband's family. The philandering prince was at the centre of another marriage scandal in 1876, when Lord Aylesford threatened to divorce his wife for her affair with Lord Blandford, the elder brother of politician Lord Randolph Churchill. The latter intervened to protect the family honour by threatening to reveal the details of compromising letters written to Lady Aylseford by Bertie unless the prince persuaded his compliant friend Lord Aylesford to drop the legal action. This ugly blackmail attempt so incensed the prince that he sought to resolve the matter by means of a pistol duel with Churchill who laughed off the challenge.

The Prince of Wales could not avoid another court appearance when he forced Sir William Gordon-Cumming to sign an undertaking that he would never gamble again after being caught cheating at baccarat in 1891. The culprit agreed to the ultimatum on condition that the matter was kept quiet, but when the secret was leaked and openly discussed in social circles, he sued five people for slander and called the heir to the throne as a witness. Gordon-Cumming lost the case, was dismissed from the army and expelled from his clubs, while the prince's public image was severely damaged for encouraging illegal gambling.

The researches of Andy and Sue Parlour as told to author Kevin O'Donnell in *The Jack the Ripper Whitechapel Murders* (1997) develop an earlier contention by John Wilding in *Jack the Ripper Revealed* (1993) that Bertie and some of his friends kept a room above a butcher's shop in Watling Street, City of London, where they regularly changed clothes to go fire-watching. It is proposed that the property was also used for wild orgies with prostitutes and, following a dinner celebrating his Silver Wedding Anniversary in March 1888, while Princess Alex and Queen Victoria went for a coach ride around the city, the prince was given a surprise treat by his rakish chums who took him to the secret address for a romp with Mary Kelly, who subsequently claimed to be carrying his child. To suppress the impending royal scandal and save the monarchy, a high-ranking cabal involving Prime Minister **Lord Salisbury**, chief of police **Sir Charles Warren**, and the prince's recently reconciled friend **Lord Randolph Churchill**, resulted in the killing of Kelly's known associates carried out by trusted aides, Montague Druitt and **James Kenneth Stephen**. The Parlours believe that the body whose face was badly disfigured at Mary Kelly's lodging house was some other unfortunate soul and that the woman carrying the royal baby was possibly saved by her lover who heard of the plot and spirited her out of the country to Canada.

The Prince and Princess celebrated their Silver Wedding Anniversary in 1888.

This highly speculative scenario is underpinned by the baffling contention that the bodies of the women were placed in a position pointing towards the Houses of Parliament and some coins found by one the corpses were facing upwards showing the face of Queen Victoria, which, with the ritualistic mutilations of the victims, suggest a link with the Freemasons whose Grand Master was the Prince of Wales. Bertie never acknowledged the existence of any illegitimate children, although it was widely rumoured that he had sired a child by Lady Susan Pelham-Clinton therefore, why would he suddenly have a twinge of conscience for a common whore like Mary Kelly, when her story of impropriety could have been dismissed as the rantings of a madwoman and dealt with as easily as the earlier allegations made by the conveniently certified Lady Mordant?

3

Joseph Merrick
(1862-1890)

THE ELEPHANT MAN

The Deadly Fruit of Original Sin.

FREAK-SHOW SIGN ADVERTISING
JOSEPH MERRICK IN WHITECHAPEL

Early in December 1886, *The Times* published a letter from the Chairman of London Hospital, Frederick Carr Gomm, making a heartfelt plea on behalf of 'an exceptional case' – a man whose disfigurement was so 'dreadful a sight' that the writer declined to shock readers with a detailed description of his infirmities, other than to say that he was referred to as 'the elephant man', adding:

> Terrible though his appearance is, so terrible indeed that women and nervous persons fly in terror from the sight of him, and that he is debarred from seeking to earn a livelihood in any ordinary way, yet he is superior in intelligence, can read and write, is quiet, gentle, not to say even refined in his mind.

The patient, Joseph Merrick, was born in Leicester and, during infancy, developed a rare condition, believed to be Proteus syndrome, which twisted his body and caused the skull tissue to swell enormously with the skin resembling a huge brown cauliflower. Following the death of his mother when he was nine, his father remarried and the boy was treated so badly by his stepmother that he left home to be cared for by an uncle until forced to enter the workhouse for a period of four years.

By 1884, Merrick, now aged twenty-two, realised his only hope of escape from the horrors of the poor law, lay in becoming a novelty in a 'freak show' and wrote to a local music hall owner, Sam Torr, who agreed to promote his appearances. After touring the Midlands, the show transferred to the capital where Merrick was being exhibited in a vacant shop opposite London Hospital in Whitechapel, when the 'Elephant Man, half-a-man, half-an-elephant' came to the attention of one of the medical establishment's most eminent surgeons Dr Frederick Treves, who took a personal interest in the hideously deformed young man and presented him for examination to members of the Pathological Society.

Moved on from London by the authorities who denounced the freak show as an outrage against public decency, Merrick took up an offer to appear in Belgium where he was robbed and abandoned by his newly acquired Austrian manager. Pawning any items of value he possessed, he raised enough money to pay his passage back to England and sought sanctuary with the only person he felt he could trust, Dr Treves. Hospitals for 'incurables' refused to accommodate Merrick, even when the management of London Hospital offered to pay for his care, however, thanks to the generosity of *The Times* readers, sufficient funds were raised to enable him to remain in specially converted rooms at London Hospital. Here he became something of a *cause celebre* receiving visits from several charitable aristocratic ladies. His most distinguished guest was Princess Alexandra, whose husband the **Prince of Wales** knighted Dr Treves for services rendered shortly after succeeding to the throne as King Edward VII upon the death of **Queen Victoria**. The king urgently required surgery for appendicitis in June 1902, but strongly opposed going into hospital. 'I have a coronation on hand', he protested. But Treves was adamant: 'It will be a funeral, if you don't have the operation'. The king heeded Treves's persuasive argument and the ceremony was temporarily postponed while the troublesome abscess on his appendix was successfully drained. Ironically, the surgeon honoured for saving the monarch, subsequently suffered a burst appendix while living in retirement at Lausanne, Switzerland, dying from peritonitis in December 1923, having recently completed a book *The Elephant Man and Other Reminiscences*.

Dr Treves and Joseph Merrick, a classic personification of the fictional Dr Jekyll and Mr Hyde portrayed in the contemporary stage production by actor **Richard Mansfield**, have both been implausibly denounced as suspects in the hunt for Jack the Ripper. With not a

Joseph Merrick, 'half-a-man, half-an-elephant'.

Dr Frederick Treves.

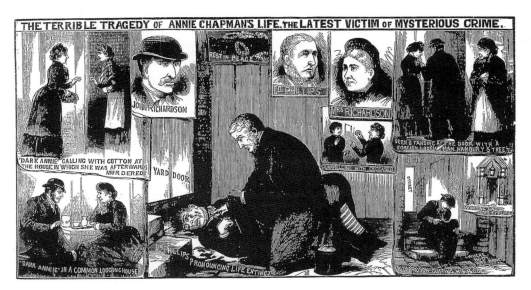

The Whitechapel Murders occurred in the vicinity of London Hospital.

shred of tangible evidence against either man, the only reason for them being recently named on a true crime website appears to emanate from the fact that they were conveniently based in Whitechapel. The requisite attributes of a murderer from a respectable background with anatomical knowledge were possessed by Treves, who once famously denounced the presence of 'a plague of women' attending the wounded while serving as consulting surgeon to the British Army during the Boer War. His celebrated patient, the 'Elephant Man' always carried a picture of his mother as a reminder of the only female who had shown him any love, therefore, his experience with other women who found him repulsive supposedly developed into a bitter hatred and, with surgical knives readily available in the hospital, provided the means and an adequate motive to carry out the gruesome attacks.

The 'Elephant Man' passed away aged twenty-seven, just eighteen months after the last of the recognised Whitechapel Murders — a good time to die for a Ripper suspect — and it has been proposed that, racked with guilt over his terrible crimes, he decided to end his miserable existence and commit suicide. An inquest found that his sudden and unexpected death was caused by suffocation when it appeared that he had attempted to fall asleep laying down, whereas his condition usually forced him to prop himself upright to support his head and slumber in comfort. Had Merrick been the Ripper, the sight of a severely afflicted figure with a pronounced limp, who covered his deformities in public with a long flowing theatre cloak and netting hung from a huge yachting cap, would surely have been noticed by the hordes of plain-clothes policemen and members of assorted vigilance committees who roamed the streets specifically looking to apprehend suspicious-looking characters. If any other alibi were needed, it is accepted that the victim's throats were slashed by a right-handed killer, which would have been absolutely impossible for Merrick as this limb was grotesquely enlarged and rendered useless — as explained by Frederick Carr Gumm who confirmed in his letter to *The Times* that 'only one arm is available for work'.

4

Richard Mansfield
(1857-1907)

The Strange Case of Dr Jekyll and Mr Hyde

An actor must pretend to be what he is not; he must be what he pretends to be.

RICHARD MANSFIELD

The elusiveness of Jack the Ripper created a widely held belief that Jack the Ripper was a gentleman cloaked in respectability by day who metamorphosed into a murderous fiend at night. Eerily, at the outset of the serial murder scare, such a character was being portrayed on the London stage in *The Strange Case of Dr Jekyll and Mr Hyde*.

The stage adaptation of Robert Louis Stevenson's horror novella, that had become popular on both sides of the Atlantic, starred famous actor-producer Richard Mansfield. Born in Berlin, the son of soprano Erminia Rudersdorff and London wine merchant Maurice Mansfield the budding actor was educated in England, then, having also inherited his mother's musical talent, established himself in his chosen profession appearing in many of the D'Oyle Carte company's productions of Gilbert & Sullivan's comic light operas. He created the role of the Major General in a bizarre world premier of *The Pirates of Penzance*. To establish copyright for the composers, the players read from their scripts while dressed in their everyday clothes during a secretly arranged one-off performance before an audience of less than fifty people at the aptly named Bijou Theatre, in the seaside resort of Paignton, Devon.

Following the death of his mother in Boston, Mansfield moved to the USA in 1882 and became an American citizen after establishing himself on the New York stage. Following the publication of Stevenson's best seller in 1886, Mansfield obtained the rights to the story and, with a script by playwright Thomas Russell Sullivan, enjoyed considerable success with the production in his adopted homeland, before making a triumphant return to London where he was engaged to appear in the dual role by the greatest thespian of the age, Sir Henry Irving, lessee of the Lyceum Theatre. The show opened early in August and reviews of the melodrama were enthusiastic and fulsome in their praise of the histrionic performance. The *Daily Telegraph* critic wrote, 'Mr Mansfield triumphed. He has come, he has seen, he has conquered', while the *Daily News* dubbed the portrayal, 'A creation of genius' and predicted that 'the town will flock to see it'. Audiences were thrilled and astounded at Mansfield's frightening ability to transform himself, in the words of *The Times* reviewer, from the 'bland and somewhat platitudinous, philanthropist' Dr Jekyll, into the 'crouching, Quilp-like creature, a malignant Quasimodo, who hisses and snorts like a wild beast' while satisfying his lust for violence as the repulsive Mr Hyde. The character's change was brought about by drinking a powerful chemical potion and achieved by the actor with a quick change on a darkened stage enhanced by no more than a natural ability to change the muscles in his face, the tone of his voice and the posture of his body. Mansfield's friend and fellow actor De Wolf Hopper once asked for a demonstration while the two men were talking in the Continental Hotel, Philadelphia, 'And then and there, only four feet away, under the green light, as that booming clock struck the hour – he did it – changed to Hyde before my very eyes – and I remember that I, startled to pieces, jumped up and cried that I'd ring the bell if he didn't stop'. The effect on unwary audiences was even more electrifying and it was recorded by biographer Paul Wilstach in *Richard Mansfied: The Man and the Actor* (1908), that 'Strong men shuddered and women fainted and were carried out of the theatre … People

Richard Mansfield as Dr Jekyll and Mr Hyde.

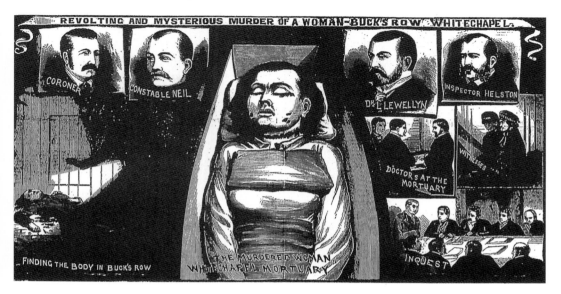

The death of the first victim Mary Nichols coincided with the opening of Mansfield's play.

went away from Dr Jekyll and Mr Hyde afraid to enter their houses alone. They feared to sleep in darkened rooms. They were awakened by nightmares. Yet, it had the fascination of crime and mystery, and they came again and again'.

Although the play would be considered tame by today's standards, Victorian sensibilities were shocked, yet, drawn by the current fashionable interest in the occult to Stevenson's morbidly compelling psychological study. However, four weeks after opening at the Lyceum, fact and fiction suddenly became blurred by events in Whitechapel. Fear gripped the capital as the body count of mutilated prostitutes grew and Mansfield's production was hysterically accused in the press of encouraging serial murder. Despite responding to the outcry by putting on a special benefit performance to raise funds to open a laundry employing reformed prostitutes, audiences dwindled and, after a run of only eleven weeks, the show was forced to close before the end of October.

Inevitably, rumours circulated connecting Richard Mansfield to the crimes. Scotland Yard was swamped with letters naming suspects from members of the public, including one from a disturbed theatre-goer who was tormented by the harrowing performance he had witnessed and could not believe that an actor could be so convincing in a stage role without being a murderer in real life, alleging that the American must be Jack the Ripper. This view of Richard Mansfield as a suspect was compounded in the 1988 television series *Jack the Ripper*, a drama documentary starring Michael Caine as investigating police officer Inspector Abberline, which portrayed Mansfield (played by Armand Assante) as a man who frequently availed himself of the services of prostitutes in the East End. There is no evidence to support this claim and the scenario is unlikely, as during the London run, the actor was romancing Beatrice Cameron, a member of his company whom he married in 1892. Furthermore, his only brush with the law seemingly occurred in New York, where he was arrested and charged with 'disorderly conduct' in 1896, for ignoring a policeman's request to stop riding a bicycle on a concourse reserved for carriages in Central Park.

Reminiscing to the *New York Times* in October 1913, actress Margaret Wycherly added some credence to the case against Mansfield when she recalled him as a gruff, irritable, eccentric character who totally immersed himself in his roles:

The player that really feels and enters into his part, is truly a very rare object. But Mr Mansfield was one that actually seemed a changed man. Nights when he played 'Dr. Jekyll and Mr. Hyde', the whole company remained away from him, players, stage manager, and manager.

5

Charles Parnell
(1846-91)

THE UNCROWNED KING OF IRELAND

We presume that anyone who ever followed the career of
Mr Parnell or admired him will cling to the belief that the
frantic follies of his last years were the result of disease, and not a
revelation of long-hidden unsoundness.

OBITUARY IN *THE NEW YORK POST*, 7 OCTOBER 1891

In October 1888, *Judy*, the sister magazine of *Punch*, published a satirical article that cleverly interlinked the two big news stories of the day – the agitation for Irish Home Rule and the hunt for Jack the Ripper. In the story, 'Paddy' was on trial for the 'attempted mutilation' of his employer Mrs United Kingdom, an elderly, domineering woman, who showed 'few signs of decay'. Despite providing him with a livelihood and lavishing fringe benefits on him for many years, the ungrateful Paddy sought freedom to make his own decisions and was demanding an independent lifestyle. Ignoring the maternal interest of his employer, her many kindnesses were forgotten as he lured her into 'a dark passage of her own history' whereupon she was brutally attacked and mutilated 'by cutting off a portion of her anatomy called Ireland'.

In the political climate of the day, it was thought within the bounds of possibility, that the Whitechapel Murders were the latest acts of terrorism to be carried out by Irish nationalist fanatics. Previous atrocities had included the dynamite outrages of 1885 when explosions caused extensive damage to Scotland Yard and the House of Commons. Three years earlier, the Irish Invincibles, a group funded by London-based Fenians, admitted responsibility for the assassination of Lord Frederick Cavendish, the newly appointed British Chief Secretary of Ireland, and his deputy, Thomas Burke, as they strolled unguarded to their residences in Phoenix Park, Dublin. In a scene reminiscent of the fate that was in store for the unfortunate victims of the Ripper, shocked witnesses looked on in horror as the defenceless men were slashed and mutilated with long double-edged knives. A police officer rushed to the scene of the heinous crime and discovered the bodies of the politicians lying in pools of blood on the roadside. Terrible wounds had been inflicted on Thomas Burke, denounced by nationalists as the leading 'rat' in the British 'occupation'. He was stabbed repeatedly in the back, neck, chest and pierced through the heart, before his windpipe was savagely severed. Frederick Cavendish rushed forward in a vain attempt to protect his colleague and struck one of the two assailants across the face with his umbrella calling him a 'ruffian' before running into the road where he was savagely attacked and suffered a broken arm and cuts to his hands and face in trying to ward off blows, before a deadly blade was plunged into his side, neck and lungs. As he fell to the ground he was almost struck by two passing cyclists who hurriedly pedalled out of harm's way as they heard the mortally wounded man cry out, 'Ah! You villain'.

Four days earlier, Prime Minister **William Gladstone** had made concessions to the Irish Nationalist Party and released their leader Charles Parnell, who had been held in Kilmainham Gaol for six months for making 'violent speeches' against repressive government policies and inciting agrarian violence by encouraging tenant farmers to 'boycott' unpopular landowners. The new political deal was seriously jeopardised by the merciless killings, with Gladstone's own niece now the tragic widow of his protégé and former private secretary Frederick Cavendish.

Charles Parnell publicly denounced the Phoenix Park murders, but the incident returned to haunt him in May 1887 when *The Times* published damaging allegations implying his involvement. The series of articles upset the alliance of the Liberal Government and the Irish Nationalist party, who were now both committed to the concept of Home Rule. The House of Commons established a special parliamentary commission to investigate the level of responsibility for terrorist activities attributable to Parnell. In February 1889, the long-running inquiry questioned shady Irish political journalist Richard Pigott who confessed to having

Charles Parnell.

Parnell's 'dream' of an Irish Parliament was put on hold while accusations of terrorist links were investigated by a special commission.

The divorce scandal which ruined Parnell's career.

forged letters reproduced in *The Times*, purportedly written by Charles Parnell, which falsely implied that the politician condoned the assassinations. Even the commission judges laughed at the hapless forger when he was unmasked by failing a simple test that trapped him into repeating spelling mistakes that had appeared in the fake correspondence.

Proclaimed the 'Uncrowned King of Ireland' and totally exonerated of any complicity in the spate of violent acts in London and Ireland by the report of the Parnell Commission, the party leader's standing had never been higher as he was afforded immense respect in Britain and America. However, his career and any immediate hopes of Home Rule for Ireland were soon to be destroyed by further ruinous scandal. Richard Piggott, fearing arrest after being tricked into giving his incriminating testimony, fled abroad to Madrid. When the police turned up at his hotel, the desperate journalist seized a revolver from his suitcase, put the muzzle to his mouth and blew his brains out. Coincidentally, the man who had shadowed the fugitive and summoned the authorities was Captain William O'Shea, whose estranged wife Katherine had been Parnell's lover for several years and had given birth to three children by him. In 1888, newspaper editor **William T. Stead** had mischievously hinted in the *Pall Mall Gazette* that Parnell was spending a lot of time at the O'Shea's London home, and it may have been the publicity and the resultant social embarrassment that goaded the cuckolded captain into initiating divorce proceedings. In December 1889, Parnell was cited as co-respondent and did not defend the action, acknowledging the depth of the illicit relationship by later marrying the object of his adulterous affections. However, the damage to his personal reputation and political career was irreparable. The Irish parliamentary party split in disarray over the question of his suitability to lead them and he was forced to resign. Spurned by his party and the public, Charles Parnell enjoyed less than four months of married life, before suffering an heart attack brought on by a bout of rheumatic fever, passing away in his wife's arms at the age of forty-five. The momentum of his partnership with William Gladstone in working towards a solution to his country's 'troubles' had been crucially stalled by the orchestrated smear campaign in *The Times* which, it later emerged, had been anonymously written by a Home Office civil servant and former Irish secret agent, **Robert Anderson**, who was soon to be appointed head of the Criminal Investigation Department and charged with the task of apprehending the elusive Jack the Ripper.

6

Lord Salisbury
(1830-1903)

An Honest Politician

A gram of experience is worth a ton of theory.

LORD SALISBURY IN *SATURDAY REVIEW*, 1859

Upon the retirement of revered politician Benjamin Disraeli in 1881, the Right Honourable Robert Arthur Talbot Gascoyne-Cecil, the third Marquess of Salisbury, became leader of the Conservative Party and during the next decade secured three terms of office as Prime Minister. His lordship's second administration from 1886-1892 was embarrassed by the emergence of the first internationally renowned sexual serial killer - later giving rise to tales that the premier was involved in a cover-up of, either a royal marriage scandal or, an Irish republican plot, to conceal the true motive of the murders credited to the mythical Jack the Ripper.

The royal conspiracy theory crystallised in Stephen Knight's *Jack the Ripper: The Final Solution* (1976) contends that Mary Kelly, having witnessed the secret marriage of Prince Albert Victor the **Duke of Clarence** to shop-girl Annie Crook, attempted to blackmail the government with a group of East End harlots. The Prime Minister, shocked that the heir presumptive had taken a Catholic bride, feared for the future of the monarchy and enlisted fellow Freemason, **Lord Randolph Churchill**, to recruit **Sir William Gull**. The royal physician, ably assisted by artist **Walter Sickert** and coachman John Netley, saved the nation by successfully tracking down and purging the country of the treasonous whores.

In reality, Salisbury's strict religious and moral beliefs would have prevented him from countenancing such a proposal. He had not been afraid to display stern opposition to the philandering lifestyle of Albert Edward the **Prince of Wales**, by habitually banning his mistresses from visiting his private residence Hatfield House. The phrase 'honest politician'– often cynically viewed as a contradiction in terms – is an apt description of the Tory premier. Furthermore, neither Churchill nor Salisbury were Freemasons and, in any case, such drastic action by a

Lord Salisbury.

Catholic Home Secretary Henry Matthews.

secret society was not necessary, for, having been arranged without the sovereign's permission, the alleged marriage could have been annulled under the terms of the Royal Marriages Act 1772.

The use of this institutional Anglican legal mechanism was potentially embarrassing for the royal family and would have stirred up even more resentment among Irish Catholics who were conducting a campaign of violence against what they perceived as unwarranted occupation of their homeland by the British. The Irish 'problem' had dominated the 1886 General Election, which, had been lost by the ruling Liberal Party, when Prime Minister **William Gladstone** campaigned on the sole issue of granting Home Rule to Ireland. His minority government had depended on the support of the Irish Nationalist Party led by **Charles Parnell**, who held the delicate balance of power in the House of Commons. The 'Home Rule' policy was vehemently opposed by incoming Tory Premier, Lord Salisbury, who, by way of appeasement appointed Henry Matthews, the first Roman Catholic government minister of cabinet rank since the Elizabethan age, to the post of Home Secretary. The new Secretary of State's reward was to be saddled with the major headache of solving the mystery of the killings attributed to Jack the Ripper. Recent evidence, presented by author Nick Warren in an essay *The Great Conspiracy* (1999), suggests that Matthews was successful, although the results of the inquiry were suppressed for reasons of political expediency. Warren recounts, how in the 1970s, Ripperologist Donald Rumbelow was presented with what is reputedly 'Jack the Ripper's knife' by a lady who had obtained it in 1937 from Major Hugh Pollard, an associate of Robert Churchill, a former Scotland Yard ballistics expert and Intelligence Officer to the Chief of Police in Dublin during the 'troubles'. Although the exact provenance of the knife cannot be established, the handle of the weapon indicates it was purchased from John Weiss & Son, the instrument makers of Bond

Street, London. The length of the blade has been truncated but, quite clearly, was originally the same make and type of 12in double-edged amputating knives, which were used in the political assassinations of Lord Frederick Cavendish and Thomas Burke. Twelve of the long surgical knives had been smuggled across the Irish Sea disguised as false pregnancies beneath the skirts of female sympathisers. Only three of the weapons were recovered by the police from the perpetrators of the horrific crime, the self-styled Irish Invincibles, whose avowed intent was 'To make history and to remove the principal tyrants of the country'.

Nick Warren highlights the idiosyncratic choice of such knives as evidence of a plot for a ritual murder by the secret society and speculates that the government of the day, led by Lord Salisbury, called a truce with representatives of the Fenian movement, brokering a deal in which the investigation into the deaths of five prostitutes would be called off in return for a cessation of terrorist activities. The problem with this intriguing theory and the assertion that the same weapons were used in Dublin and London is that, according to gang leader James Carey – who avoided prosecution by turning Queen's evidence against his fellow conspirators – most of the knives were disposed of by breaking the blades into pieces and burning the handles. More significantly, no Irish republican organisation claimed responsibility for the Whitechapel Murders as they had for the Phoenix Park atrocity. In fact, the authorities had no clue to the identity of the assailants until they themselves sought credit for their despicable act by delivering black-edged cards to newspaper offices bearing the words 'Executed by order of the Irish Invincibles'.

The Phoenix Park Murders.

7

Lord Randolph Churchill
(1849-1895)

THE FOURTH PARTY

Churchill is the Dr Jekyll and Mr Hyde of modern politics.

PALL MALL GAZETTE, 22 JUNE 1886

Lord Randolph Churchill had a meteoric career in British politics. A brilliant and controversial orator who made friends and enemies in equal measure, he was appointed Chancellor of the Exchequer and Leader of the House of Commons. Ranked in importance alongside Prime Minister **Lord Salisbury** and his predecessor **William Gladstone**, it seemed only a matter of time before he would follow these illustrious names and occupy the ultimate seat of power. However, all was lost when the ambitious young politician reacted rashly to opposition from fellow ministers to his proposed defence cuts by offering his resignation in December 1886. He gambled that his popularity would rally support from the Cabinet who would beg him to stay, but the ploy failed spectacularly when he was allowed to step down and his life in the limelight was effectively over as he slid into obscurity and a premature grave suffering from syphilis of the brain.

Churchill had been cast into the social and political wilderness once before after deeply offending the **Prince of Wales** in 1876. During an official visit to India, the prince's hunting companion Lord 'Sporting Joe' Aylesford received a letter from his wife informing him that she was carrying another man's child and that she intended to elope with the father, Randolph's married elder brother, the Marquess of Blandford. Forced by the impending scandal to cut short the wholesale slaughter of elephants and tigers on the sub-continent, the cuckolded husband travelled back to England threatening to turn his gun on his love rival and let it be known that his friend the prince regarded the man who had stolen his wife as 'the greatest blackguard alive'.

Randolph Churchill intervened to try and save the reputations of all concerned and persuaded the love-struck couple to drop their plans to set up home together. In the meantime, 'Sporting Joe', unable to track down the target of his revenge, instigated divorce proceedings

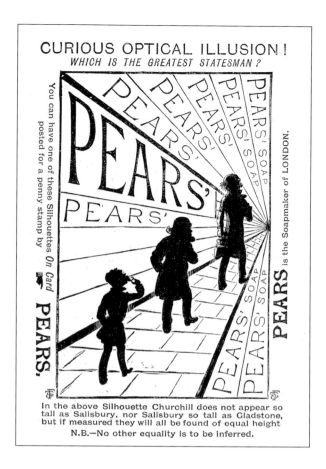

CURIOUS OPTICAL ILLUSION!
WHICH IS THE GREATEST STATESMAN?

You can have one of these Silhouettes *On Card* posted for a penny stamp by

PEARS'

PEARS' is the Soapmaker of LONDON.

In the above Silhouette Churchill does not appear so tall as Salisbury, nor Salisbury so tall as Gladstone, but if measured they will all be found of equal height

N.B.—No other equality is to be inferred.

that precipitated an ugly blackmail attempt upon the heir to the throne. Obtaining a collection of admiring letters written by the Prince of Wales to Lady Aylesford, Churchill called on the Princess of Wales and told her that 'being aware of peculiar and most grave matters affecting the case, he was anxious that His Royal Highness should give such advice to Lord Aylesford as to induce him not to proceed against his wife'. He shocked the princess by informing her that the letters were 'of the most compromising character' and warned he had legal assurance that the prince would be subpoenaed to give evidence if the divorce case continued and that if published, the letters would ensure that 'His Royal Highness would never sit upon the Throne of England'.

The Prince of Wales reacted to this outrageous conduct by dispatching his aide, Lord Beresford, to London with instructions to request Churchill to name his seconds for a duel where the law would turn a blind eye to the outcome on the north coast of France. Churchill declined the invitation to attempt to kill the heir to the throne and taunted the prince for issuing a challenge, knowing full well it was impossible to accept. The row escalated until Lord Aylesford bowed to pressure to renounce his divorce plans and Churchill reluctantly proffered a half-hearted apology to the prince for dragging his name into the sorry episode. Having been so insulted, it was no surprise when the Prince of Wales responded by making it known he would never enter a house in the kingdom that welcomed Blandford or Churchill. The disgrace of the affair forced the brothers' father, the Duke of Marlborough, to accept an invitation from sympathetic Prime Minister, Benjamin Disraeli, to leave the country and become Lord Lieutenant of Ireland, with Randolph accompanying him to Dublin to serve as unpaid private secretary.

The social ostracism of the family lasted eight years before the Prince of Wales accepted an invitation engineered by Randolph's wife Jennie Jerome, a charming hostess who claimed to have invented the 'dinner party of deadly enemies'. The American beauty is thought to have enjoyed an affair with the future king, after physical relations with her husband were curtailed when he displayed secondary symptoms of a sexually transmitted disease contracted in his youth. By this time, Churchill's political star was rising, although Queen Victoria, who had wholeheartedly supported her son's position during the unpleasant interlude, denounced his appointment as Chancellor of the Exchequer describing him as 'so mad and odd'. In 1884, Churchill had founded the influential 'Fourth Party', the nickname of a radical democratic group of Tories committed to reforms giving greater power to the rank and file. It has also been alleged that he became the 'fourth party' in the Whitechapel Murders, when the government asked the fallen politician to supervise the elimination of women who knew about the secret marriage between the **Duke of Clarence** and a common shop girl, Annie Crook. According to further revelations from Joseph Gorman Sickert recorded by author Melvyn Fairclough in *The Ripper and the Royals* (1991), Churchill was the highest Freemason in the land and recruited a trio consisting of **Sir William Gull**, the physician's footman Frederico Albericci and a coachman, John Netley, to ritually murder the women as a patriotic duty.

Apart from the obvious contradiction of a man who once boasted he had the Crown of England in his pocket, suddenly being relied upon to save the monarchy for his arch enemy the Prince of Wales and, furthermore, accepting the request from Premier, Lord Salisbury, the man who had left his political career in ruins after unexpectedly accepting his resignation 'with profound regret', there is absolutely no evidence to support the claim that Randolph Churchill was a Freemason – although the organisation later attracted the distinguished membership of his son and future Prime Minister, Sir Winston Churchill.

Lord Randolph
Churchill.

8

Sir Charles Warren
(1840-1927)

HOUNDED OUT OF OFFICE

The police force a failure,
Rotten at the core;
Their 'beats' are a failure,
In this age of gore.
By Warren's strange decree
Our Criminals are free,
And England is daily on the tremble.

JUDY, 10 OCTOBER 1888)

Knighted for a distinguished military record, Sir Charles Warren resigned from the Army to stand unsuccessfully as an Independent Liberal candidate in the 1886 General Election. His political ambitions thwarted, he was immediately offered and accepted the position of Metropolitan Police Commissioner. He had proved his aptitude for the post in 1882, when he was sent to Egypt to discover the fate of Professor Edward Palmer's archaeological expedition. The entire party had been robbed and murdered, yet, Warren recovered the victims' remains then sought out the criminals and brought them to justice.

Warren's brief tenure at Scotland Yard was to prove controversial. In November 1887, he deployed 4,000 policemen, 300 soldiers and 600 mounted police and life guards to disperse 100,000 unemployed demonstrators marching to hold a banned rally in Trafalgar Square. Violent clashes resulted in the death of one man and a further 150 people were hospitalised in a heavy-handed operation remembered as 'Bloody Sunday'.

The police chief's ineffectual handling of the Whitechapel Murders was to speed his downfall. Endlessly mocked in the popular press for his failure to apprehend Jack the Ripper, Warren was also ridiculed for conducting trials with bloodhounds in Hyde Park. Their owner Edwin Brough had

Sir Charles Warren.

trained two magnificent animals, Champion Burnaby and Burgho, to follow the trail of a man in the dark in the manner that would be necessary if employed to pursue the killer through the East End. Sir Charles witnessed the trials and volunteered to act as the hunted man with the hounds baying at his heels. Derided as a publicity stunt, the dogs were not purchased when they disappeared in the fog during further trials on Tooting Common and, in an ironic role reversal, the police were called in to track down and find the missing bloodhounds. A month after this embarrassing episode, Warren's tendered his resignation on 9 November – the day that Mary Kelly's horrifically mutilated body was found – a leader in the *Star* triumphantly crowed, 'Whitehall has avenged us for Bloody Sunday'.

In *Jack the Ripper: The Final Solution* (1976), author Stephen Knight proposed that far from being an abject failure, Warren was highly successful in his prime objective to conceal the identities of those responsible for the five Whitechapel Murders. In Knight's account, at the time of the atrocities, the police commissioner was one of the country's highest ranking Freemason's and thereby compelled to assist any senior member of the brotherhood to escape punishment for any crime – however heinous. In the summer of 1885, while visiting the Cleveland Street studio of artist **Walter Sickert**, Prince Albert Victor, the **Duke of Clarence** was introduced to a Roman Catholic shop girl Annie Crook. Soon the prince was not only sowing 'wild oats' but also the 'seeds of revolution' as the couple began a passionate affair. Annie fell pregnant and the following April gave birth to a daughter christened Alice, before a looming national crisis

Casting off.

The arrival of Sir Charles Warren.

Inspecting the dogs

Sir Charles Warren hunted.

In Full Cry.

At Fault.

Crossing the drive

Louis Wain.

The finish to the hunt.

Burgho

Barnaby

The Bloodhounds used in the Trials

Bloodhounds track down Charles Warren in Hyde Park.

was created when they entered into a secret marriage. The relationship was doomed from the moment a furious **Queen Victoria** learned of her grandson's scandalous conduct and a sharply worded note to Prime Minister **Lord Salisbury** instigated a cover-up. The Freemasons were enlisted to murder friends of the bride who were attempting to blackmail the government with knowledge that she had been removed to an asylum by secret agents, which, threatened the very existence of the monarchy, therefore, royal physician, **Sir William Gull** was recruited and instructed to ritually disembowel the treasonous females. On the day that the first killing occurred, another prominent Freemason, Dr **Robert Anderson**, took over the office of assistant commissioner, personally appointed by Warren to oversee the investigation into the Whitechapel Murders. Suspiciously, Warren insisted that no one should approach a crime scene without his express permission and after the 'double event' ordered the removal of cryptic graffiti scrawled on a wall near the body of Catherine Eddowes which read, 'The Juws are the men that will not be blamed for nothing'. The news of the chalked message brought Sir Charles scurrying into Whitechapel for the first time and he forbade the taking of photographs explaining that he feared anti-Jewish riots sparked off by the reference to 'Juws'. Knight argues that this was not a misspelling – for the 'Juws' were the three apprentice Masons who unlawfully killed Hiram Abiff, the chief architect of Solomon's Temple that forms the very basis of Masonic ritual.

Stephen Knight justified his marvellously weaved conclusions by suggesting that only Warren's supremacy in Freemasonry seems to explain his appointment as commissioner as the grave situation was developing in 1886, for, he had no relevant background in police work. However, this argument is not borne out by the facts. Warren's appointment was generally welcomed and *The Times* commented that he was 'precisely the man whom sensible Londoners would have chosen to preside over the police of the Metropolis'. Furthermore, Warren's resignation was not made because it was mission accomplished once the final victim had been eliminated in a Masonic plot, but because senior civil servants reprimanded him for responding to press criticism of his force by writing an article for a magazine that had not been cleared for publication by the Home Office. Warren's indignant departure to rejoin the Army was purely a response to wounded pride and the worst that he can be accused of is fumbling incompetence in the fruitless search for Jack the Ripper.

9

The Duke of Clarence (1864-92)

THE PRINCE OF DARKNESS

[Prince Eddy] seems to inherit his father's vices without retaining many of his virtues.

DAILY NORTHWESTERN (USA), 1890

For generations Queen Victoria's grandson Prince Albert Victor, the Duke of Clarence was *persona-non-grata* in royal circles – despite the fact that only an early death prevented him from fulfilling his destiny to be crowned King of England. Familiarly known as Prince Eddy, his name has resurfaced in recent times as the subject of unsavoury involvement in sex scandals and the hunt for Jack the Ripper, explaining perhaps, why he had been airbrushed from history.

A royal conspiracy theory attributes the Whitechapel Murders to people acting in Prince Eddy's interests. In a dramatised BBC investigation aired in 1973, Joseph Gorman Sickert, purporting to be the illegitimate son of eminent artist **Walter Sickert**, claimed his father had a studio in Cleveland Street, where he gave art lessons to Prince Eddy. During these visits, the prince met and fell in love with a girl called Annie Crook who worked in a nearby tobacconist's shop. In 1885, the couple were secretly married and had a baby daughter named Alice. The Establishment were horrified when they learned of the young royal's involvement with a commoner who was also a Catholic. Early in 1888, Prince Eddy was ushered abroad and in his absence his unsuitable 'wife' was forcibly committed to an asylum where an operation performed by royal physician **Sir William Gull** wiped out her memory of the event. Baby Alice had been left in the care of Annie's friend Mary Jane Kelly, who had witnessed the marriage and now feared for her safety at the hands of the authorities. Leaving Walter Sickert to look after the child (who later in life allegedly became his lover and the mother of Joseph), Mary Jane took refuge in the East End, where she confided in a group of female friends and together they hatched a plot to extort money from the government in return for their silence. Faced with a

Prince Albert Victor.

national emergency and the prospect of the downfall of the monarchy if the story came out, the Prime Minister, **Lord Salisbury**, enlisted the help of the Freemasons. They in turn ordered Sir William Gull to deal with the problem by knifing and ritually disembowelling the blackmailers. Ripperologists have dismissed this highly imaginative story by citing legislation which would have made Prince Eddy's marriage to a Catholic invalid and prevented the child of such a union from succeeding to the throne. Apart from having to ride out a tirade of possible sensational newspaper headlines, if details of the wedding were true, there was no necessity to be concerned about a blackmail attempt. However, convincing proof that prostitutes successfully blackmailed Prince Eddy over another matter was exposed when a letter to his solicitor, George Lewis, came up for auction in 2002. Writing in 1891, the prince complained about the exorbitant expense of paying off one of the loose women in return for some compromising correspondence:

I am very pleased that you are able to settle with Miss Richardson, although £200 [£12,000 today] is rather expensive for letters. I presume that there is no other way of getting them back without paying that sum. I will also do all I can to get back the one or two letters written to the other lady. You may be certain that I shall be careful in the future not to get into any more trouble of this sort.

Prince Eddy was also implicated in another scandal involving Cleveland Street, when a number of his aristocratic friends were arrested during a police raid on the brothel where they engaged in sex acts with telegraph boys in 1890. One of those apprehended was Lord Arthur Somerset who escaped prosecution when he threatened to implicate the heir presumptive in the matter unless he was allowed to slip away into exile. However, the assumption that Prince Eddy was a homosexual is questionable as in the wake of the Cleveland Street 'rent boy' scandal, he precipitated a constitutional crisis by contemplating giving up his right to the throne for a love match with his Catholic French cousin Princess Helene d'Orleans, before arrangements were hastily made for his betrothal to a suitable Protestant bride, Germany's Princess Mary of Teck. Tragedy struck before the wedding could take place when the prospective groom passed away aged only twenty-seven in January 1892. His heartbroken fiancée quickly recovered from the shock and merely transferred her affections to Eddy's younger brother whom she subsequently married and reigned alongside as Queen Mary when he ascended to the throne as King George V in 1910 (the royal couple are the grandparents of Elizabeth II).

In another 'Ripper' scenario, first proposed by Dr Thomas Stowell in an article 'Jack the Ripper – A Solution?' published in the *Criminologist*, (November 1970), Sir William Gull's presence in the East End is explained away by the intimation that he was searching the area trying to apprehend and certify the insane Prince Eddy who was doubling as Jack the Ripper. The official cause of the prince's premature death was given as pneumonia, although there has been speculation that this was a by-product of syphilis of the brain, brought about by his relationships with prostitutes which prompted him in his madness to go on the rampage in

Ceremony installing Clarence as Grand Master of Berkshire Freemasons.

Lord Arthur Somerset.

Whitechapel. When exacting his revenge and removing organs from his victims he utilised skills learnt while hunting and dressing deer. A royal cover-up ensued when Prince Eddy confessed to the murders under hypnosis and with the agreement of his father, the **Prince of Wales** and, the Prime Minister, Lord Salisbury; an overdose of morphine was administered to bring an end to a brief and iniquitous life. Alternatively, it was suggested by author Melvyn Fairclough in *The Ripper and the Royals* (1991), that the story of the deranged prince's death was concocted to hide the fact that he had been secretly locked away at Glamis Castle where he survived until the 1930s. This version of events has been conclusively disproved. In 1892, the prince's body had been displayed lying in state and court records give Prince Eddy convincing alibis for his whereabouts on the dates when the killer struck. The royal suspect was well outside London, at either Sandringham or locations in Yorkshire and Scotland, during the entire reign of terror, which, makes nonsense of persistent claims that he eliminated women, engaged in the world's oldest profession from whom he had supposedly contracted a then incurable sexually transmitted disease.

10

Sir William Gull
(1816-1890)

Physician Extraordinary

It was said that on more than one occasion Sir William Gull
was seen in the neighbourhood of Whitechapel on the night of
a murder.

DR THOMAS STOWELL IN 'JACK THE RIPPER
– A SOLUTION?' *CRIMINOLOGIST*, NOVEMBER 1970

With **Queen Victoria** in prolonged mourning following the death of her husband Prince Albert, the future of the monarchy was soon in serious crisis. The heir apparent, the **Prince of Wales** played no useful role in state affairs and his life was spent socialising at music halls, yachting regattas, hunt meetings and racecourses. The notorious womaniser was booed several times in public following his humiliating appearance in the divorce court where he was forced to deny having an affair with the wife of Sir Charles Morndaunt in 1870.

The royal family's deep unpopularity evaporated the following year when the prince was struck down with typhoid and the Queen was informed that his death was imminent. A wave of public sympathy accompanied the month-long battle against the killer disease and the remarkable change in attitude was noted by the London correspondent of the French newspaper *Le Gaulois*:

Here we have the spectacle of a real nation kneeling to the Almighty and praying that the days of their future sovereign may be prolonged. This England, which we were told, was ready to become a Republic, which was accused of despising its princes, and having got rid of all its old-fashioned ideas of loyalty – come and see it today, note its grief, and be instructed.

The prince's life remained in danger until the fever broke just before Christmas and the Prime Minister William Gladstone capitalised on the situation by persuading the Queen to attend a service of thanksgiving at St Paul's Cathedral in February 1872. All thoughts of republicanism were forgotten as the royal party was heartily cheered through the streets of London. The prince's saviour had been his Physician-in-Ordinary, Dr William Withey Gull, who was knighted and created a baronet for his crucial role in the royal patient's recovery – acknowledged by a grateful sovereign in this bulletin from Sandringham published in the press:

> In Dr Gull were combined energy that never tired, watchfulness that never flagged – nursing so tender, ministry so minute, that in his functions he seemed to combine the duties of physician, dresser, dispenser, valet, nurse – now arguing with the sick man in his delirium so softly and pleasantly that the parched lips opened to take scanty nourishment on which depended the reserves of strength for the deadly fight when all else failed, now lifting the wasted body from bed, now washing the worn frame with vinegar, with ever ready eye and ear and finger to mark any change and phase, to watch face and heart and pulse, and passing at times 12 or 14 hours at that bedside. And when that was over, or while it was going on – what a task for a physician! – to soothe with kindest and yet not too hopeful words hers whose trial was indeed great to bear, to give counsel against despair and yet not to justify confidence.

Sir William Gull was also immediately appointed Physician Extraordinary to Queen Victoria and, according to several Ripper theorists, saved the monarchy once again when he was called upon to eliminate females with knowledge that Prince Albert Victor, the **Duke of Clarence** had married commoner Annie Crook, who had borne his child. Gull was not actually named in connection with the Whitechapel Murders until November 1970, when an article appeared in the *Criminologist* written by Dr Thomas Stowell, a former junior partner of Gull's son-in-law

The Prince of Wales was saved from death by Dr Gull.

Sir William Gull.

Dr Theodore Dyke Ackland. In conversations with Gull's daughter, Caroline Ackland, Stowell learned that Lady Gull had been deeply upset by a visit from a medium accompanied by the police. According to author Frank Spiering in *Prince Jack* (1978), this claim was supported by a diary entry of Gull's deposited at the New York Academy of Medicine, although a subsequent search by staff found no such evidence. In the 1973 BBC Drama Documentary, *Jack the Ripper*, which was elaborated upon in Stephen Knight's best-selling book *Jack the Ripper: The Final Solution* (1976), Joseph Gorman Sickert asserted that he had learned from his father **Walter Sickert** that Mary Kelly was a witness to the secret marriage of Prince Albert Victor and with a number of friends attempted to blackmail the government. The Prime Minister, **Lord Salisbury**, responded by engaging Sir William Gull to murder Kelly and her accomplices – utilising his surgical skills to mutilate the bodies with Masonic symbolism for their betrayal. When renowned spiritualist **Robert James Lees** allegedly had a vision which led to the arrest of Gull, the elderly physician was incarcerated in an asylum, his death announced and a mock funeral arranged in January 1890 – to prevent the embarrassing details of the royal conspiracy being revealed in a court case.

A distinguished medical career has been besmirched with these false allegations, for, at the time of the East End Murders, Sir William Gull was seventy-one years old and, had recently suffered two debilitating strokes that, rendered him incapable of practicing medicine. His death was brought about by a third seizure and, as his condition deteriorated for two days, pressmen observed several carriages conveying people to his home to pay their final respects. Contradicting the theories devoted to his role in a series of murders he was physically incapable of committing, his pathetic last words were written on a piece of paper and handed to his valet 'I have no speech'.

II

Sir Robert Anderson
(1841-1918)

The Third Man

If nonsense were solid, the nonsense that was talked and written about those murders would sink a Dreadnaught.

SIR ROBERT ANDERSON

Jack the Ripper first struck on 31 August 1888 and on that fateful day when Mary Ann Nichols became the first victim of the Whitechapel Murders, Dr Robert Anderson was appointed Assistant Commissioner of the Metropolitan Police Criminal Investigation Department. Barely a week later, the official was diagnosed as suffering from 'overwork' and granted sick leave. He travelled to recuperate in Switzerland on the day that the killer struck again, claiming the life of Annie Chapman. Following the double murder of Elizabeth Stride and Catherine Eddowes, Anderson was recalled from the Continent to take personal charge of the investigation and later claimed that he stopped the murders after the death of Mary Kelly by the simple expedient of telling prostitutes to look out for themselves as the police would no longer protect them. Believing that it was the responsibility of the police to enforce morality, he thought the episode was sensationalised beyond all reason in the press, commenting that 'the wretched victims belonged to a very small class of degraded women'.

Anderson's absence from the country may have been a tactical withdrawal as it also coincided with the opening of a Parliamentary Special Commission investigating a libellous series of articles which he had anonymously submitted to *The Times* in 1887, falsely accusing Irish Nationalist leader **Charles Parnell** of involvement in the recent dynamite outrages in London and the violent deaths of Lord Frederick Cavendish and Thomas Burke in Dublin, political victims of the Phoenix Park Murders in 1882. Parnell advocated Home Rule for Ireland, a stand not acceptable to the ruling Conservative Party under **Lord Salisbury**, who did not wish to relinquish central power nor, republican extremists, who demanded nothing less than full independence for the Emerald Isle.

Lord Frederick Cavendish – a victim of the Phoenix Park Murders.

Born in Dublin, Robert Anderson trained as a barrister before being recruited for secret service work attached to the Home Office in London. From 1865-87, he accumulated unrivalled knowledge of the republican movement and obtained intelligence of terrorist campaigns from agents including the famous American Fenian spy Thomas Beach. Although Anderson's superiors subsequently denied any knowledge of his attempt to discredit Parnell, his actions took pressure off the government over the burning issue of Home Rule – a proposal supported by Liberal opposition leader **William Gladstone**. Anderson avoided detection and the special commission took several months to clear Parnell of complicity in terrorism and the wronged politician was awarded £5,000 in a libel action against *The Times*.

In 1901, Anderson retired from Scotland Yard and was knighted. In his memoirs *The Lighter Side of My Official Life* (1910), he admitted his role in the Parnell affair and in the same volume Anderson stated as a 'definitely ascertainable fact' that Jack the Ripper had been positively identified as a 'Polish Jew':

> During my absence abroad the Police had made a house-to-house search for him, investigating the case of every man in the district whose circumstances were such that he could go and come and get rid of his blood-stains in secret. And the conclusion we came to was that he and his people were low-class Jews, for it is a remarkable fact that people of that class in the East End will not give up one of their number to Gentile Justice.

In 2006, a copy of Anderson's memoirs was presented to the Black Museum at Scotland Yard. It had been personally owned by Anderson's assistant in the hunt for the Ripper, Chief Inspector Donald Swanson, who in the margin scribbled 'the suspect was Kominski'. A Polish-Jewish hairdresser living in Whitechapel, Aaron Kominski, was taken to a workhouse infirmary in 1891,

Sir Robert Anderson.

then an asylum where he died in 1919. Regarding an unnamed Jewish eyewitness who identified Kominski, Swanson added 'Because the suspect was also a Jew and also because his evidence would convict the suspect and witness would be the means of murderer being hanged – which he did not wish to be left on his mind'.

Although it has been clearly established beyond doubt that Dr Robert Anderson was on the Continent during the 'double-event' killing of two prostitutes, he was named as the 'third man' who supposedly assisted royal physician **Sir William Gull** and coachman John Netley in a Masonic plot approved by **Lord Salisbury**, to slay the women attempting to blackmail the government with knowledge that Prince Eddy, the **Duke of Clarence** had married shop-girl Annie Crook. The child of this secret union, Alice Crook, married a man named Gorman and subsequently gave birth to a son named Joseph, who later learned he had been illegitimately fathered by artist Walter Sickert. Joseph Gorman Sickert's 'rambling saga' of a royal, governmental and Masonic conspiracy related to him by his alleged father, appeared in *Jack the Ripper: The Final Solution* (1976). Although the best-selling book's author Stephen Knight, believed high-ranking Freemason Dr Robert Anderson's behaviour at the height of the Whitechapel Murders was highly suspicious, deserting his post to go on holiday while a homicidal maniac was on the rampage, his watertight alibi made him 'the most unlikely of the three men named to have been connected with the Ripper'. Knight then proceeded to upset his elderly, confused informant by deducing that the 'third man' was none other than the man who had imparted so much knowledge of the affair – Walter Sickert – who, apart from not divulging his key part in the murder plot was suddenly 'transformed from a dubious story-teller' into the one man in the long history of Ripperology 'who had spoken the truth, the whole truth and nothing but the truth'.

12

Walter Sickert (1860-1942)

JACK THE RIPPER'S BEDROOM

It is certain that people with guilty secrets do suffer from a compulsion to drop clues, as Sickert claimed to have done in his paintings.

PSYCHOLOGIST DR ANTHONY STORR IN *JACK THE RIPPER: THE FINAL SOLUTION,* 1976

The undisputed leader of the London impressionist movement, artist Walter Sickert was born in Munich, the son of a Danish father and English mother. In 1869, the family settled in London and after completing his formal education, Walter studied acting under the world-famous thespian Sir Henry Irving, before switching to art as a pupil and assistant of the recognised master of avant-garde, James McNeil Whistler. Developing his own style by 1888, Sickert matched his mentor's fame by drawing inspiration from his first love, the theatre, depicting life in the capital's seedy music halls. French impressionism merged with realism, as sleazy lodging houses became another favourite topic for his brushes, fuelled by the artist's obsession with crimes of violence, particularly the Whitechapel Murders.

Amused by children who chanted 'Jack the Ripper' at him as he walked by them in the street, Sickert thereafter produced paintings wearing a red scarf that he claimed had belonged to a Ripper victim. He also regaled people with a tale of how

Walter Sickert.

he had rented a room in 1905 which, his landlord and landlady told him, had been previously occupied by a 'pale veterinary student' who fell ill and was collected by his widowed mother in the middle of the night shortly after the horrific mutilation of Mary Kelly. The lodger had been in the habit of staying out all night and burning his clothes on his return before rushing out to buy the morning newspapers, leading the couple to conclude that their tenant was none other than Jack the Ripper. Sickert recreated this room on canvas and entitled it *Jack the Ripper's Bedroom*.

Some theorists believe that other paintings by Sickert give subtle clues suggesting that he knew who was responsible for the East End Murders. He produced several variations of a fully clothed man and woman in the work *Ennui*, with a different picture on the wall in the background. In one, a young woman is depicted with a man lurking behind her in the shadows, while in another the painting is of a statute of **Queen Victoria**, with a seagull perched on her shoulder. These have been imaginatively interpreted as a reference to a royal conspiracy involving the sovereign's physician **Sir William Gull**. In *Jack the Ripper: The Final Solution* (1976), Stephen Knight recounted the amazing story of Joseph Gorman Sickert who claimed to be the illegitimate son of Walter Sickert and the grandson of Prince Eddy, the **Duke of Clarence**. The woman destined to be the Ripper's final victim had witnessed the wedding ceremony and fled to the East End when the authorities tried to hush up the matter by abducting her friend Annie Crook. Kelly and her co-plotters were subsequently eliminated when they made a clumsy attempt to blackmail the government. Walter Sickert's painting of *The Camden Town Murder* – seemingly based on the case of a woman whose throat was cut as she lay in her bed, for which, one of the artist's models Robert Wood was tried and acquitted in 1907 – has an alternative title *What Shall We Do For the Rent?* which, Sickert informed his son was a depiction of Mary Kelly, whose body was discovered by a man calling to collect rent arrears.

Joseph Sickert also learned from his father that Sir William Gull, coachman John Netley and CID chief **Robert Anderson** were recruited by the Freemasons to ritually disembowel the women with a dangerous secret. However, Stephen Knight concluded that Walter Sickert, not Robert Anderson, was the 'third man'. Young Alice Crook was raised by friends of Sickert then married an impotent man named William Gorman before having a long-term affair with the artist resulting in the birth of Joseph Gorman Sickert. This highly complex and ingenious scenario is totally unsupported by documentary evidence and was discredited by Joseph Sickert himself when he confessed to having 'made it all up'. He then produced three diaries purporting to have been the property of investigating officer Inspector Frederick Abberline. Information from this source appeared in *The Ripper and the Royals* (1991) alleging that **Lord Randolph Churchill**, John Netley, Sir William Gull and the physician's footman Frederico Albericci executed the plan to preserve the secret of Prince Eddy's foolhardy marriage to a shop girl, although the book's author Melvyn Fairclough later acknowledged that he no longer believes the diaries to be genuine, perhaps, prompted by his informant's claims that he frequently took tea with the queen!

Jean Overton Fuller in *Sickert and the Ripper Crimes* (1990) claimed that the artist acted alone based on the reminiscences of his friend Florence Pash who told the author's mother that she believed Sickert must have seen the bodies as he described their injuries graphically in conversation. Further evidence pointing the finger of guilt at Sickert was presented by successful American novelist Patricia Cornwell who published the findings of a multi-million dollar

Sickert was in Dieppe during the 'London Murder Scare'.

investigation in *Portrait of a Killer* (2002). Disturbed by the nature of the artist's paintings of naked women in bedrooms, the author set out to prove that he was a serial killer who claimed the lives of up to forty women. Joseph Gorman Sickert's claims to be his illegitimate son have never been established and the painter's three marriages were childless, which, Cornwell proposes, was due to a fistula of the penis, rendering him impotent and thereby the act of murder became his only means of achieving sexual fulfillment.

All the stories relating Walter Sickert's complicity in the Whitechapel Murders have been refuted by his biographer Matthew Sturgis. In *Walter Sickert: A Life* (2005), he revealed that, when the first four victims of the Ripper were slain, the artist was staying with his mother and brother in the Dieppe area of France. His presence there from mid-August until early October 1888, is confirmed by a number of letters, including one from his mother to a relative stating that they were all having a 'happy time'. Although it was technically possible for Sickert to make marauding ferry trips across the English Channel, Sturgis concludes that Patricia Cornwell's attempt to justify her case against Sickert is, like her best-selling novels, 'pure fiction'.

13

King Leopold II
(1835-1909)

THE BARBARIC BEAST OF THE BELGIAN CONGO

Ought King Leopold to be Hanged?

W.T. STEAD IN *THE REVIEW OF REVIEWS*, SEPTEMBER 1905

Succeeding his father to the Belgium throne in 1865, King Leopold II proclaimed that 'all that I desire is to leave Belgium larger, stronger, and more beautiful'. The constitutional monarch had no say in government policy and when politicians ignored his pleas to increase the country's influence and become a colonial power, the sovereign obtained a government loan to purchase his own private kingdom in Africa. His subsequent reign of terror would rival the evil exploits of the world's most barbarous dictators, Joseph Stalin, Adolph Hitler and Attila the Hun.

In 1885, representatives of America and fourteen European countries attended the Conference of Berlin to carve up the Dark Continent for economic exploitation. Leopold was granted sovereignty over an area seventy-six times larger than Belgium, which, is now known as the Democratic Republic of Congo. Leopold had prepared his application well, having previously funded two expeditions by Henry Morton Stanley. The famous explorer mapped the region and bartered for treaties with 450 tribal chiefs who unwittingly signed away all rights to their lands in exchange for a few baubles and trinkets.

Leopold presented himself as a philanthropist undertaking to protect the interests of the indigenous population by stamping out border raids by Arab slave traders, only to enslave the entire nation himself for personal gain. Forced labour was used to exact a vast fortune from the lucrative world trade in ivory and rubber that was exported from the country along trade routes established by his American envoy Henry Morton Stanley. A private army, the Force Publique, comprising of native conscripts led by European officers, ruthlessly crushed any opposition and occupation leader Leon Rom displayed the rotting heads of rebels on the picket fence of his garden, which also had a rockery built from the skulls of victims. His soldiers were

King
Leopold II.

ordered to prove their success by bringing back a dead person's right hand for every bullet fired, forcing them to cut off the hands of the living to ensure that the total tallied with the number of spent cartridges. This gruesome policy was featured in the poem *The Congo* by American Vachel Lindsay:

> Listen to the yell of Leopold's ghost,
> Burning in Hell for his hand-maimed host

The brutal regime came under close scrutiny in 1895, when an Englishman, Charles Stokes, was arrested for illegal trading, then summarily tried and hung the next day. During the early 1900s, international opposition grew and writer Mark Twain branded Leopold a 'greedy grasping, avaricious, cynical, bloodthirsty old goat', while, the editor of the *Review of the Reviews*, **William T. Stead**, expressed the opinion that Leopold should be brought to justice for his crimes against humanity and face the death penalty before an international tribunal at the Hague. The bad publicity surrounding the atrocities affected Leopold's popularity in his homeland and, he survived an assassination attempt from an anarchist who fired three shots at the royal carriage, as the sovereign was returning from a memorial service for his recently deceased wife in 1902. The king further scandalised society during the period of official mourning by openly flouting his lover Blanche Delacroix aka Caroline Lacroix, a former prostitute who subsequently bore him two illegitimate sons. In 1909, the king suffered a crippling stroke and as he lay on his deathbed he married his mistress. Five days after the wedding, he passed away and outraged subjects loudly booed the State funeral cortege through the streets.

Henry Morton Stanley founder of the
Congo 'Free' State.

During a period of a quarter of a century, the consequences of forced labour and atrocities committed in Leopold's name had reduced the population of his private domain from an estimated thirty million to less than ten million in, what **Sir Arthur Conan Doyle** described as, 'the greatest crime in all history'. Genocide had been perpetrated on a people systematically 'robbed of all they possessed, debauched, degraded, mutilated, tortured, murdered, all on a scale as has never, to my knowledge, occurred before in the whole course of history'.

Prior to his coronation, Leopold had visited London where he was allegedly a valued client of a flagellation house at Hampstead. Against this background, he was proposed as a suspect for the Whitechapel Murders by Jacquemine Charrot-Lodwidge, a researcher employed by Daniel Farson the author of *Jack the Ripper* (1972). The theory is founded on nothing more than idle speculation that the king's taste for prostitutes and sadistic tendencies gained from witnessing the atrocities in the Congo, plus the possibility that he may have been the high-ranking personage supposedly apprehended at a house in London by **Robert James Lees**, even though the identity of the medium's suspect has been generally assumed, from the clues presented in press revelations, to be royal physician **Sir William Gull**, who allegedly went on a killing spree to cover-up the potentially damaging marriage of a commoner to the queen's feckless grandson and heir presumptive, the **Duke of Clarence**. The proposition against Leopold is completely groundless as the cruel dictator ruled by decree and never travelled to the Congo, nor, made any official visits to England in 1888, therefore, it is patently obvious that he did not expand his murderous domain and 'reign' over the East End of London as Jack the Ripper.

14

Robert James Lees
(1849-1931)

THE HUMAN BLOODHOUND

Robert James Lees ... is the person entitled to the credit of tracking Jack the Ripper.

SUNDAY TIMES-HERALD, CHICAGO, 28 APRIL 1895

The hue and cry surrounding the Whitechapel Murders had long died down when a sensational story surfaced in America asserting that the perpetrator of the crimes had been apprehended by a well-known spiritualist who had utilised his 'extraordinary clairvoyant powers' to lead the police to the home of a 'great West End physician'. Although the name of the murderer was withheld, there were many clues to his identity in the story, broken in Chicago by the *Sunday Times-Herald* in April 1895, that revealed how spiritualist Robert James Lees was 'the gentleman to whom the unfortunate of the east end of London owe their present immunity from the attacks of a monster'.

Described in the newspaper article as 'the recognised leader of the Christian Spiritualists in Great Britain', the 'gift' of Robert James Lees, had been recognised at the age of nineteen, when, according to his own unverified claims, he was summoned before **Queen Victoria** during a royal visit to Birmingham. There he conducted a séance which 'excited her majesty's utmost astonishment' by relaying messages from the spirit of her dear departed husband Prince Albert. After working as a journalist on the *Manchester Guardian*, Lees moved to the Capital and at the height of the Ripper scare, he contacted Scotland Yard having experienced visions of the killer at work. His diary records that the police regarded him as just one of many 'cranks' that had been bombarding them with ideas and theories on how to catch the killer.

The Chicago newspaper article explained that police perceptions changed when Lees was travelling down Oxford Street on an omnibus and 'experienced a singular sensation' about a fellow passenger. Leaning over to his wife he remarked earnestly, 'That is Jack the Ripper!'

She laughed nervously at his dreadful suggestion and told him not to be foolish. 'I am not mistaken,' replied Lees, 'I feel it.' At this point the man in question alighted at Marble Arch and, bidding his wife to continue on her journey home, Lees followed the man down Park Lane. Half way along the thoroughfare he met a constable and implored him to arrest the 'Ripper'. Unsurprisingly, the constable ignored his request and threatened to 'run him in.' Meanwhile, the suspect realised he was being followed and escaped by jumping into a cab. Lees hastened to Scotland Yard, and voiced his suspicions to an inspector who consented to allow the medium to try and track down the fugitive. Utilising his awesome powers, Lees guided a posse of police through the streets of London throughout the night until the exhausted 'human bloodhound' closed in on his prey and halted at the gates of a mansion where he announced convincingly, 'There is the murderer – the man you are looking for.' The incredulous inspector ordered a search of the house that uncovered incriminating evidence against the owner 'a celebrated physician' who broke down and admitted his guilt, begging to be killed at once, as he 'could not live under the same roof with such a monster.' Secretly confined in an asylum in Islington, a sham death and funeral of the doctor was enacted and all London mourned his untimely 'death'.

It is universally assumed that the medium's target was royal physician **Sir William Gull** whose death occurred in 1890. However, there are no police records to support that Lees had any involvement in the investigation and some Ripper buffs have dismissed the Chicago story as a hoax perpetrated by English members of a private club in Chicago, although the idea may well have been planted there by Lees' close friend, **William T. Stead** – the world's best-known journalist – who had campaigned extensively on social conditions in the 'Windy City'. Supporters of Lees can point to the undeniable fact that within weeks of the startling press revelation, he closed down the People's League – a successful benevolent society that aided the poor. Its founder curiously left London for 'health reasons' – aged forty-five, although he was to survive to become an octogenarian. Although no proof of any settlement was ever produced, his spiritualist daughter Eva perpetuated her father's version of events that he had been sworn to secrecy granted a royal

Robert James Lees.

Lees claimed to have led the police to the 'Whitechapel Monster'.

pension then advised to relocate to avoid further press attention. Following spells residing in St Ives and Plymouth, Lees made his home in Ilfracombe and concentrated on writing novels with the aid of his 'spirit guide'. Late in life he returned to his native Leicester where he passed away leaving only circumstantial evidence of any connection with the celebrated murder case. Certainly, Lees and his family of sixteen children suffered severe financial hardship for many years prior to 1888, when his fortunes were mysteriously restored just months after the last of the Whitechapel Murders. In addition to the alleged pension from the Privy Purse, he led people to believe that he received a substantial reward for apprehending 'Jack the Ripper' – a windfall that enabled him to pursue philanthropic activities that had to be abandoned when the newspaper article citing his involvement in the murder investigation appeared in 1895. Lees privately confirmed to all and sundry that he deserved the credit for solving the case. His obituary revealed that he had also recently spoken to the press on the matter without identifying the villain, whose name he continued to withhold even when contacted through séances beyond the grave:

> Mr Robert James Lees … claimed to be the only surviving person who knew the identity of Jack the Ripper … Some months ago, he told a Leicester Mercury man that he offered his services to Scotland Yard, with a view to tracing the criminal … Mr Lees made the astounding statement … that he actually enabled the Yard to associate with the crime, a man who died in a lunatic asylum. (*Leicester Mercury*, 12 January 1931)

15

William T. Stead
(1849-1912)

SHOCK JOURNALISM

*That man has done more harm to journalism than any other
individual ever known.*

WILLIAM GLADSTONE ON WILLIAM T. STEAD

Sensational bold headlines, pictorial illustrations and provocative leading articles were pioneered by journalist William Thomas Stead – editor of the influential *Pall Mall Gazette*. The newspaper was an organ of the Liberal Party led by William Gladstone, who was to later regret recommending Stead for the post, as the new editor was a leading exponent of the 'new journalism' or 'shock journalism', agitating for social reforms and endeavouring to make the newspaper 'the tribune of the poor'.

The crusading editor took a proactive approach and his finest piece of investigative journalism appeared in July 1885 when he exposed the horrors of child prostitution in London. In a series of articles entitled 'The Maiden Tribute of Modern Babylon' he described how he had bought a thirteen-year-old girl from her willing mother to demonstrate how easily the depraved lust for a virgin could be satisfied in the sex trade. The campaign forced the government to swiftly introduce legislation raising the age of consent to sixteen years and earned Stead the lasting respect of Salvation Army leader **General William Booth** with whom he helped to ghost write *In Darkest England and the Way Out* (1890). However, the authorities reacted to the manner of the scandalous revelations by having Stead arrested on trumped up charges of abducting a minor without her father's consent, for which, he was sentenced to three months imprisonment. On each anniversary of this blatant miscarriage of justice, Stead would proudly appear in public wearing a prison uniform.

Prostitution was also at the heart of the story of the Whitechapel Murders and the *Pall Mall Gazette* accepted pieces on the crimes by Robert Donston Stephenson. The freelance writer

William T. Stead.

who styled himself Dr Roslyn D'Onston, had a chronic drink and drug dependency problem and, in November 1888, while receiving treatment for neurasthenia at the London Hospital in Whitechapel, claimed to have seen Dr Morgan Davies disgustingly demonstrating how the women were sexually assaulted. When allegedly told by William Stead that the final victim Mary Kelly had been sodomised, Stephenson informed Scotland Yard that he was convinced, from the mime he had witnessed, that Davies was Jack the Ripper. However, as no such sex act took place, Dr Davies was not questioned by the police. In 1890, Stephenson himself became a suspect, when he told business associate Baroness Vittoria Cremmers that the Ripper concealed the organs removed from his victims in a box of neckties, not realising that she had seen some blood encrusted ties in Stephenson's room. The baroness revealed the story many years later to journalist Bernard O'Donnel and in 1929, a variant published in the *East Anglican Daily Times* by Pierre Girouard made the unsubstantiated claim that Stephenson had confessed his guilt on his deathbed in a New York Hospital. Author Melvyn Harris in *Jack the Ripper: The Bloody Truth* (1987), also speculated that Stephenson approached the police to deflect suspicion from himself and concluded that he was the killer as the murders came to a halt when his health broke down.

William Stead briefly had his own suspicions about Stephenson, though his interest in psychic phenomena and close friendship with **Robert James Lees**, suggests that he knew far more about the rumours of the involvement of the spiritualist whose renowned 'gift' supposedly helped the police to secretly apprehend **Sir William Gull**. In 1895, the story of Lees identifying 'a great West End physician' as Jack the Ripper was revealed by a newspaper in Chicago, probably mischievously planted there by Stead who, for the previous two years, at the invitation of local dignitaries, had personally conducted a crusade for civic reform after attending the World Fair in Chicago. If there had been any truth in the tale, the astute journalist would not have passed up the opportunity of publishing such a 'scoop'.

Stead often predicted that his own death would come about by drowning and it came to pass that he lost his life while travelling to speak at a peace conference in New York on the ill-fated liner *Titanic*. The impending maritime disaster and his tragic fate had been addressed in his writings. In his book on spiritualism *How I Know the Dead Return*, one paragraph begins 'Let

The sinking of the *Titanic*.

us consider the Atlantic as the grave'. The author then compares one shore with Earth and the other with the Eternal shore. In March 1886, he published a fictitious article entitled *How the Mail Steamer Went Down in Mid-Atlantic, by a Survivor*. In the story an unnamed steamer collides with another ship and due to a shortage of lifeboats there is a huge loss of life. Stead comments 'this is exactly what might take place and will take place if liners are sent to sea short of boats'. Uncannily, the event that sent him to a watery grave was graphically prophesised twenty years before his death in an article published in the December 1892 issue of the *Review of Reviews* – an international monthly magazine founded by him. In a tale entitled 'From the Old World to the New', Stead describes how a White Star liner, the *Majestic*, is carrying a group of English tourists across the Atlantic to visit the World Fair in Chicago when, one of the passengers, a clairvoyant, picks up a telepathic message from a friend who is close to death and floating helplessly in the water having survived the wreck of the *Montrose*, sunk after colliding with a giant iceberg that can be seen from the *Majestic*. The clairvoyant persuades the captain to put him out on a boat and his powers guide him to rescue the survivor. The setting of the story and the descriptions of the iceberg and the wrecked ship tally almost exactly with the fate of the *Titanic* – although by 1912, Marconi's wireless telegraph, not telepathy, sent an SOS to summon the rescue boat *Carpathia*.

In the midst of the biggest news story of the century, the journalist calmly helped women and children into the lifeboats, secure in his belief in spiritualism that there was nothing to fear from death. He had expressed his opinion on the matter only two months earlier in a letter of condolence to his recently bereaved friend Robert James Lees:

I am so sorry that you have lost your wife or rather that she is no longer with you in her physical presence.

You have consolations which others have not, and I have no doubt that you have already heard from her since she passed over to the other side.

16

Aleister Crowley
(1875-1947)

THE WICKEDEST MAN IN THE WORLD

All London was discussing the numerous problems connected with the murders; in particular it seemed to everybody extraordinary that a man for whom the police were looking everywhere could altogether escape notice in view of the nature of the crime.

ALEISTER CROWLEY ON
THE INVISIBLE POWERS OF JACK THE RIPPER

Occultist and author of several books on the art of black magic, Aleister Crowley, dropped out from Cambridge University in 1898, to join the Hermetic Order of the Golden Dawn, a quasi-secret society influenced by the principles of freemasonry and theosophy who initiated an 'elite' band of men and women into the mysteries of alchemy and the occult. Believing he was the reincarnation of notable French mystic Eliphas Levi, Crowley travelled the world, furthering his knowledge of the black arts and searching for his personal 'guardian angel'. Fleeing from India to avoid a police investigation after he had shot dead two would-be assailants and, from Sicily, following the mysterious death of a disciple, such incidents led Theosophy Society and Golden Dawn member, writer W.B. Yeats, to brand Crowley 'insane' and the popular press to refer to him as 'The Beast' and 'The Wickedest Man in the World'.

Pursuing a lifestyle of drug-fuelled, black magic homosexual rituals, Crowley's marriage ended in divorce on the grounds of his adultery, although, he then proceeded to father several illegitimate children by women who provided him with financial support. Even so, having become a hopeless heroin addict, he died virtually broke. Found among his effects was an unpublished dissertation on the East End Murders which, at first glance, appears to indict the Russian founder of the theosophy movement:

It is hardly one's first guess, or even one's hundredth guess, that the Victorian worthy in the case of Jack the Ripper was no less a person than Helena Petrovna Blavatsky. She has, however, never been unveiled to the unthinking multitude; very few, even of those who have followed her and studied her intently for years, have the key to that 'Closed Palace of the King'.

Upon closer inspection of the document, it becomes apparent that Crowley merely identifies Helena Blavatsky as the catalyst or 'Star to which the persons of the drama are attached'. Significantly, the five points of a 'star' are also revealed when the sites of the five murders are joined on a map and employing astrological theory, Crowley deduced that the killer had carefully planned all the deaths to occur when the malevolent planets of Mars and Saturn were in the ascendancy – Mars being the God of magic and Saturn the God worshipped on the Witches' Sabbath.

The Whitechapel Murders occurred in 1888, the same year that the Golden Dawn was founded and **Helena Blavatsky** relocated her Theosophy Society headquarters to London. One of the latter's most fervent disciples was novelist Mabel Collins, who lived with her male lover Dr Roslyn D'Onston before she became romantically involved with lesbian American Vittoria Cremmers – the widow of Baron Louis Cremmers. Sharing Collins' house in Southsea, three soon became a crowd and the two women decided to rid themselves of the unwanted male as soon as they had recovered a collection of love-letters written to him by Collins. Searching a trunk belonging to D'Onston for the correspondence, Cremmers discovered 'five white dress ties soaked in blood'. The women then recalled an occasion when D'Onston had returned from an evening at the theatre as they were discussing the possible cannibalistic methods of Jack the Ripper. Wondering how the fiend could conceal bloodstains on his collar and tie if he had disposed of the victim's organs by eating them at the scene of the crime, D'Onston interrupted the debate and demonstrated how pulling his opera cape across his shirtfront could do this and laughingly remarked 'You see how simple it is'.

'The Beast'.

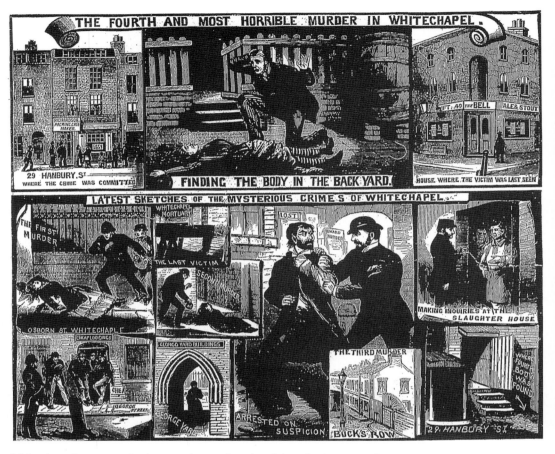

Malevolent planets were in the ascendancy when the violent deaths occurred.

The self-styled 'Dr' Roslyn D'Onston was in reality Robert Donston Stephenson who had studied chemistry, medicine and the occult, before embracing the teachings of the theosophy cult from Madame Blavatsky. From July to December 1888, he was a patient at the London Hospital in Whitechapel suffering from neurasthenia. Therefore, the only way the suspect could have slipped out and returned at night unnoticed, is by Crowley's incredulous proposal that D'Onston committed the murders and escaped detection by acquiring the power of invisibility. From his sick bed, D'Onston certainly took a keen interest in the local investigation and voiced his suspicion that the murderer was hospital doctor Morgan Davies. The *Pall Mall Gazette* also published his explanation for the cryptic message found on a wall near the body of Catherine Eddowes 'The Juwes are the men that will not be blamed for nothing' suggesting that the apparent misspelling of 'Jews' may have actually been 'Juives' indicating that the killer was a Frenchman domiciled in London.

It is clear that Aleister Crowley had no original information about the suspect. He was well acquainted with the source of his story, Baroness Cremmers, who related her experience with D'Onston to *Empire News* crime journalist Bernard O'Donnell a few years before her death in

D'Onston interpreted a cryptic message left near the body of Catherine Eddowes.

1937. She also claimed her former love rival had admitted killing the seducer of his favourite cousin, been party to the death of a Chinaman during the Californian gold rush and, once fallen in love with a prostitute who flung herself off Westminster Bridge when his family opposed their planned marriage. Cremmers learned from D'Onston that candles made from human fat were essential in the practice of black magic, together with 'a preparation made from the a certain portion of the body of a harlot'. During publication of the memoir, the *Empire News* engaged Crowley to conduct his astrological investigation. The occultist also suspected that D'Onston had written a solution appearing under the pseudonym of Tay Tria Delta in the *Pall Mall Gazette*, suggesting that a sorcerer could attain 'the supreme black magical power' by taking the course of action perpetrated by Jack the Ripper.

17

Madame Helena Blavatsky (1831-91)

JILL THE RIPPER

My Father knew the lady and, with her, would discuss wholly secular subjects; she being, he told me, one of the most interesting and unscrupulous impostors he had ever met. This with his experience was a high compliment.

RUDYARD KIPLING ON MADAME
BLAVATSKY IN *SOMETHING OF MYSELF,* 1929

At the height of the terror in Whitechapel, the Revd Lord Sydney Godolphin Osbourne suggested in a letter to *The Times* that the murderer might be a woman carrying out threats commonly uttered among streetwalkers. A fitting example of this might be 'I'll have your guts for garters'. Rumours later surfaced that a convict of Maidstone Prison had told other inmates that a hitherto dedicated nurse had exacted a terrible revenge on prostitutes after discovering that her husband had been availing himself of their services. By far the most interesting allegation of a woman's involvement was made by **Aleister Crowley**. In an article on Jack the Ripper, the black magician obliquely referred to Russian mystic Madame Helena Blavatsky, of whom the *Illustrated London News* paid this satirical tribute in her obituary:

Had she possessed a grain of honesty in her wonderfully complex character, she might have been called the most remarkable woman of the age. As she was, she acted the part of a pure charlatan, her life was largely infamous, and she had, at one time or another, played on the credulity of nearly every civilised country in the world.

Ukraine-born Helena Petrovna, the daughter of an army colonel and a novelist, clearly inherited her mother's talent for storytelling. Having toured the world, she imaginatively claimed to have

Madame Helena Blavatsky.

accomplished a great deal on her travels – utilising her incredible array of talents and abilities to become a concert pianist, a circus bareback rider, owner of an ink factory in Odessa and an importer of ostrich feathers to Paris. Simultaneously she survived a multitude of misfortunes including a shipwreck off the coast of Greece and from sabre and bullet wounds sustained while fighting for the cause of Garibaldi in Italy. She was rather less forthcoming about running a gambling den in Tiflis, although, all these real or imagined adventures paled into insignificance when she pursued a calling which was to bring her everlasting renown, due to her impressive grasp of religion, which resulted in her rejection of traditional Christian, Islam and Judaism values, in favour of the teachings of voodoo in New Orleans, Hinduism in India and Buddhism in Tibet. Soon she established a reputation as a medium practising in Cairo. Relocating to New York almost destitute, she was soon to live off the generosity of her gullible admirers when she founded the Theosophy Society in 1875. Insisting that 'theosophy' was a science not a religion, based on universal brotherhood, without distinction of race, creed, sex, caste, or colour, she declared the society was designed to promote the study of comparative religion, philosophy and science while investigating the power of the occult. These laudable ideals were destroyed when the high priestess of the new movement fraudulently proclaimed herself as the messenger of the Great White Brotherhood of Mahatmas – a celestial elite of philosophers including Buddha, Confucius, Plato, Abraham, Moses and Solomon who chose to communicate their ideas through her by 'automatic writing' or by 'materialising' to communicate with astounded audiences at theosophy society gatherings.

The leader's 'miracles' were soon exposed as a sham in India, when her Madras housekeeper, who had formerly assisted her employer with the Cairo séances, released damning letters subsequently investigated and verified by the Society for Psychical Research, which revealed the illusionist secrets of Blavatsky's supernatural manifestations. Overcoming this damaging scandal, the theosophy cult continued to expand rapidly around the globe. In 1888, its founder published a four-volume tome *The Secret Doctrine* and set up the Blavatsky Lodge in London, attracting some notable converts including writers **Arthur Conan Doyle**, **Oscar Wilde** and **William T. Stead**.

Although Madame Blavatsky was romantically linked in her youth with a German baron, a Polish prince and a Hungarian opera singer, her most ardent London disciple Annie Besant

Her manifestations were exposed as a sham.

considered that her mentor was 'much more a man than a woman … wholly different from the average female type'. William T. Stead agreed that the Russian, who swore profusely and rolled her own Turkish cigarettes, 'had the manners of a man, and a very unconventional man, rather than those of a lady' and was 'the very reverse of beautiful'. Despite these unflattering descriptions, the fraudster was believed to have entered into matrimony on three occasions – to a general aged sixty when she was seventeen (whose surname she retained), a Russian immigrant in America when she was forty-five and, a boy of sixteen when she was fifty. All the unions were brief and ended in strange circumstances. The bride fled from her first and third husbands long before the proverbial honeymoon period was over, while her 'toy boy' husband mysteriously went mad the day after the ceremony. The marriages probably failed through the spiritualist's self-confessed abhorrence of physical relationships, which contradicted allegations by her detractors that she had previously supported herself as an international *grande horizontal*. Her pent-up emotions and feelings of revulsion about sexual activity could well have provided a motive for wanting to launch violent attacks on women who made their living by such means. However, when the killer was at large, Madame Blavatsky was suffering from chronic liver disease and was so grossly overweight that her dedicated followers could only mobilise the seer by pushing her around in a bizarrely designed bath chair – rendering her incapable of committing the atrocious crimes attributed to 'Jill the Ripper'.

18

Sir Arthur Conan Doyle
(1859-1930)

THE ADVENTURES OF SHERLOCK HOLMES

You know my methods in such cases, Watson: I put myself in the man's place, and having first gauged the man's intelligence, I try to imagine how I should myself have proceeded under the same circumstances.

SHERLOCK HOLMES IN *THE ADVENTURE OF THE MUSGRAVE RITUAL*, 1893

Sherlock Holmes made his bow in *Beeton's Christmas Annual* 1887, and the following year, his creator Dr Arthur Conan Doyle applied a combination of his own medical knowledge and the cool logic of his fictional detective to the real-life case in Whitechapel. In answer to the Revd Lord Sydney Goldophin's letter published in *The Times*, Doyle responded to the churchman's notion that the killer might be female, by suggesting that a midwife (or a man so disguised) might be able to commit the murders and walk through the district in a bloodstained apron without attracting suspicion. This theory was developed further in *The Science of Sherlock Holmes* (2006), where author E.J. Wagner examined the case of Constance Kent, who, in 1860, was arrested on suspicion of murdering her four-year-old half-brother whose dumped body was found wrapped in a blanket with his throat cut right through to the vertebrae. Released without charge, the sixteen-year-old girl was sent by her family to be educated at a convent in France and five years later confessed to the crime. Because of her youth and the fact that she had given herself up, the death penalty was commuted to life imprisonment and having serving twenty years she was paroled in 1885. The book speculates that having assisted nuns to deliver babies, Constance may have used her midwifery skills to remove organs from the victims of the Whitechapel Murders, which ceased when she emigrated to pursue a successful career of nursing in Tasmania, where she died at the age of 100 in 1944.

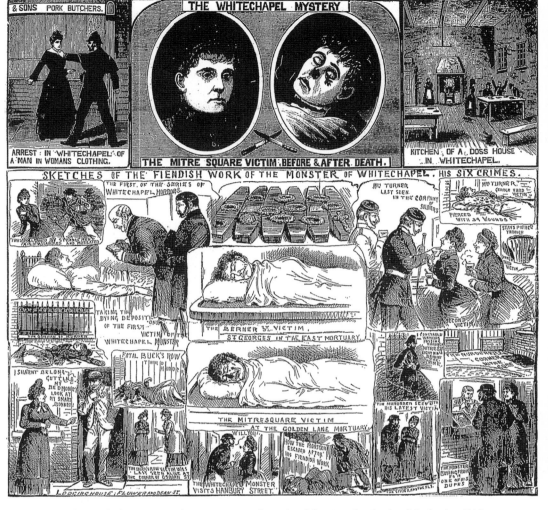

A man in woman's clothes is arrested on suspicion of murder following the death of Catherine Eddowes.

However, towards the end of his life, it appears that Conan Doyle had revised his earlier assessment about 'Jill the Ripper' and appeared to subscribe to the royal conspiracy theory when he assured Nigel Morland, the founder-editor of the magazine *Criminologist*, that the Ripper was a personage 'somewhere in the upper stratum' of society. The Sherlock Holmes investigations into *A Scandal in Bohemia* and *The Beryl Coronet* concerning the delicate indiscretions of a fictitious prince were evidently inspired by the notorious exploits of **The Prince of Wales** and **Prince Eddy**. The royal father and son would become Ripper suspects, as would Doyle who displayed a keen interest in the case by taking part in a Jack the Ripper tour at Scotland Yard. The novelist has also recently been accused of being implicated in the alleged poisoning of two male personalities. The first case occurred after Doyle returned from military medical service abroad where he drew on his personal experience to produce *The History of the Great Boer War* and a patriotic pamphlet entitled *The War in South Africa: Its Causes and Conduct* for which he was duly awarded a knighthood in 1902. Tired of the effect that crime fiction was having on his ambition to become an historical novelist; Doyle had killed off Sherlock Holmes in 1893, and then succumbed to public pressure to revive the detective hero in his best-known case *The Hound of the Baskervilles*. In the book's dedication, the author faithfully acknowledged that 'This story owes its inception to my friend, Mr Fletcher Robinson, who has helped me both in the general plot and in the local details'.

Bertram Fletcher Robinson (later editor of *Vanity Fair*) regaled Doyle with legends of spectral demon hounds while the author was staying at his home near Dartmoor in 1901. The coachman who drove the pair round the district was the man whose name inspired the title, Harry Baskerville, who later claimed that Robinson had not received the credit he deserved for co-writing the story with Doyle. In 2003, author Rodger Garrick-Steele went further in *The House of the Baskervilles* and presented a theory that Robinson was the sole author of the book and had been murdered at the insistence of Doyle who was having an affair with his wife Gladys, whom he persuaded to administer lethal doses of laudanum to her husband. Robinson was aged only thirty-six when he was diagnosed with typhoid and died in January 1907, although Doyle curiously contended that his friend, who had dabbled in Egyptology, was a victim of selective poisoning through the same so-called Mummy's Curse which later killed Tutankhamen discoverer Lord Caernavon.

Arthur Conan Doyle.

Conan Doyle had a child-like belief in the occult, believed in the existence of fairies, was a follower of the theosophy cult founded by **Madame Helena Blavatsky** and produced the *History of Spiritualism* – an issue he hotly debated in correspondence with Harry Houdini. The legendary escapologist fervently denounced false mediums until his death from peritonitis on Halloween 1926, although his great-nephew George Hardeen contended in *The Secret Life of Houdini* (2007), that no autopsy was carried out on the American showman to determine the cause of death that, he believes was an act of deliberate poisoning by a group called the Spiritualists. Among there number was Sir Arthur Conan Doyle who wrote to a fellow devotee in 1924, that Houdini 'would get his just deserts very exactly meted out ... I think there is a general payday coming soon'.

Therefore, having been sporadically accused of slashing the throats and removing the intestines of five unfortunate women, it is now suggested that the writer changed his *modus operandi* to poison two well-known men. Only an exhumation of the bodies of Bertram Fletcher Robinson and Harry Houdini will clear up the mystery of their deaths, as any noxious substances will still be detectable in their systems. Easier to resolve is the question of Doyle's involvement in the Whitechapel Murders. It is patently obvious he is in the clear, for, although the Sherlock Holmes stories are firmly associated with London and the sleuth's home at 221B Baker Street, the author was a general practitioner in Southsea, Portsmouth when Jack the Ripper was terrorising the East End. The writer only relocated to the Capital in 1891, when his popular detective stories started being serialised in *The Strand*.

19

Rasputin
(1869-1916)

GREAT CRIMINALS OF RUSSIA

No Englishman could have perpetrated such a horrible crime.

EAST LONDON OBSERVER,
9 SEPTEMBER 1888

London journalist William Le Queux covered the Whitechapel Murders for the *Globe* and some thirty years later published several books on Russia in the wake of the Bolshevik Revolution. He claimed to have possession of documents found amongst the effects of the murdered mystic Rasputin, which included an unfinished project on *Great Criminals of Russia* that named a Russian secret agent as Jack the Ripper.

The son of a Siberian peasant, Gregory Efimovich became known as Rasputin – meaning 'dissolute' – after embracing some of the more depraved doctrines of the outlawed Khlysty (Flagellants) sect which preached that only a committed sinner could be truly redeemed and that God was best communed with during the euphoria of sexual orgasm. Emerging from a brief period in a monastery at the age of eighteen, marriage a year later which, yielded four children, failed to settle the self-proclaimed holy man, who adopted a licentious lifestyle and wandered to St Petersburg, where he gained a reputation for healing the sick and predicting the future. In 1905, the coarse, unkempt 'mad monk' with the long, flowing hair and mesmerising stare answered a medical emergency when summoned to the court of Nicolas and Alexandra where, utilising his powers of hypnosis, he successfully soothed the suffering and staunched the bleeding of their haemophiliac son. Tsarina Alexandra had given birth to four daughters before producing a sole heir, the sickly Prince Alexis. When Rasputin boldly warned the parents that the health of their child and the survival of the dynasty were inextricably linked to him, they regarded the holy man as a saviour, thereby, gradually allowing him to exert a powerful influence over the imperial family and affairs of state.

Rasputin used his position as a royal favourite to satisfy his sexual appetites, seducing numerous women, who felt 'honoured' to be chosen by the preacher who convinced them that physical contact with him had a purifying effect on their spiritual wellbeing. His debauched behaviour and ability to recommend the appointment of obedient cronies to high office made him many enemies, although the tsar chose to disbelieve reports of any misdeeds by the man dubbed by his accusers, the 'Holy Devil'.

At the height of the First World War, Rasputin sensed there was a plot to kill him and towards the end of 1916 delivered a letter to Tsar Nicolas which prophesised:

> I feel that I shall leave my life before 1st January. I wish to make it known to the Russian people … If I am killed by common assassins, and especially by my brothers the Russian peasants, you, Tsar of Russia, have nothing to fear, remain on your throne and govern, and you, Russian Tsar, will have nothing to fear for your children, they will reign for hundreds of years in Russia. But if I am murdered by boyars, nobles, and they shed my blood, their hands will remain soiled with my blood … They will leave Russia … if it was your relations who have wrought my death then no one of your family, that is to say, none of your children or relations will remain alive for more than two years. They will be killed by the Russian people.

On the night of 29 December, Rasputin accepted an invitation to the palace of one of the tsar's jealous relatives, Prince Felix Yusupov, who nervously played the guitar for his guest after serving him with poisoned wine and teacakes. Two hours later, when the food and drink had not brought about the desired effect, the panic-stricken Yusupov put down the musical instrument and attempted to finish off Rasputin with a bullet in the back, then, was horrified when the 'mad monk' seemingly rose from the dead and grabbed his assassin by the throat. Yusupov broke free

A contemporary Russian cartoon lampooning Rasputin's hold over the imperial family.

Foreigners were treated with suspicion during the hunt for Jack the Ripper.

from the stranglehold and called for help. One of his fellow conspirators shot down Rasputin as the wounded man ran through the courtyard shouting, 'Felix, Felix, I will tell everything to the Tsarina'. Another bullet penetrated the skull, but Rasputin still showed signs of life and was beaten by a frenzy of blows from the club wielding Yusupov. The body was then bound and plunged through a hole in the ice in a nearby river, where their superhuman foe was finally disposed of by drowning. Within weeks the imperial regime was swept away in a revolution led by Lenin and the royal family mercilessly eliminated as had been sinisterly foretold which, coupled with the sensational nature of his death, only served to enhance the legend of Rasputin.

According to William Le Queux in *Things I Know About Kings, Celebrities and Crooks* (1923), Rasputin's papers revealed that in 1888, London-based spy Dr Alexander Pedachenko, alias Vassily Konovalov, alias Count Andrey Luiskovo, was recognised as 'the greatest and boldest of all Russian criminal lunatics' and ordered by the Russian secret service to commit the Whitechapel murders as part of a tsarist attempt to create mayhem and discredit the Metropolitan Police and the British Government, whom they believed, were too tolerant of immigrant anarchists, socialists and dissidents living in the East End. Pedachenko was assisted in his mission by a friend called Levitski, who acted as lookout, and a tailoress, Miss Winberg, who engaged the unwary prostitutes in conversation, allowing Pedachenko to sneak up and launch a frenzied attack. His mission successfully completed, the Russian Ripper then returned to his homeland, where five months later, the transvestite was arrested wearing women's clothing, charged with attempting to murder a woman and committed to an asylum where he died.

Unfortunately, neither evidence of a secret foreign plot, nor the existence of the murderer and his accomplices has been found. Furthermore, Le Queux's source material has seemingly disappeared without trace. Curiously, he claimed that the Rasputin documents had been dictated to a clerk in French, a language unknown to its alleged author, who would also have experienced great difficulty carrying out research for the proposed book on *Great Criminals of Russia* as his peasant upbringing had left him totally illiterate!

20

James Maybrick
(1838-1889)

The Diary of Jack the Ripper

It's like saying Sharon Tate was actually the Boston Strangler.

COMMENT ON SUGGESTION THAT
MURDER VICTIM JAMES MAYBRICK WAS JACK THE RIPPER
BY AUTHOR ALAN MOORE IN *FROM HELL*, 1989

Fame came too late to savour for James Maybrick, whose name first hit the headlines after he was pronounced dead with arsenic poisoning aged fifty. His young American wife Florence was charged with murder when it was discovered that she had recently purchased a large quantity of arsenic-treated flypapers and written a compromising letter to her lover saying that 'James is sick unto death'. Over a century later, evidence would emerge to suggest that this sorry episode had also put an end to the deadly activities of Jack the Ripper.

Cotton merchant James Maybrick married seventeen-year-old Southern belle Florence Chandler in 1881, having previously co-habited with a woman for several years on the fringes of Whitechapel in London. After living in the USA for three years, the Maybricks returned to England and took up residence at Battlecrease House in Liverpool. The couple had two children before matrimonial difficulties surfaced. It came as a surprise to Florence to discover that her spouse was still seeing and maintaining the long-term lover who had also borne him children. The cheated spouse promptly gained revenge by finding comfort in the arms of her husband's friend and business associate Alfred Brierley. In March 1889, the hypocritical Maybrick exploded with fury when he found out about his wife's affair and during a heated exchange gave her a black eye, then drew up a new will excluding her as a beneficiary. With his marriage crumbling, business failing and debts mounting, a more serious problem struck when James suddenly fell ill. Diagnosed with acute dyspepsia, his condition quickly deteriorated and he passed away two weeks later on 11 May.

Although the evidence against Florence Maybrick seemed damning, especially the flypapers, which she claimed, were boiled to make an arsenical cosmetic preparation, the defence contended that the deceased had been in the habit of self-administering arsenic as an aphrodisiac, which accounted for the traces of poison found in his system. This was confirmed by a post-mortem, which found arsenic in the liver, kidney and intestines, though none in the heart or blood, which would have indicated that the dead man consumed a lethal dose of poison. However, the court was totally unsympathetic with a woman who admitted adultery and the trial Judge Sir James Fitzjames Stephen (father of Ripper suspect **James Kenneth Stephen**) delivered a highly prejudicial summing up against the accused. The reason for his unbalanced ramblings soon became apparent when he was declared insane and committed to an asylum, although this was too late to help the woman in the dock whom he sentenced to death. A public outcry ensued and upon appeal the Home Secretary, Henry Matthews and Lord Chancellor Halsbury concluded 'that the evidence clearly establishes that Mrs Maybrick administered poison to her husband with intent to murder; but that there is ground for reasonable doubt whether the arsenic so administered was in fact the cause of death'. Acting on their recommendation, Queen Victoria reluctantly exercised the royal prerogative for the death penalty to be commuted to life imprisonment commenting through her secretary 'the only regret she feels is that so wicked a woman should escape by a mere legal quibble'.

Florence Maybrick gained her freedom when she was eventually released from prison in 1904. Returning to America, she compiled her memoirs *My Fifteen Lost Years* that gave no insight into her troubled marriage, merely revealing her anguish about the trial, incarceration and the unsuccessful prolonged campaign to have her case reviewed. Thereafter, she devoted her life to the welfare of schoolboys until she was found dead at her home in October 1941.

When the centenary of the Whitechapel Murders occurred in 1988, the name of James Maybrick had never been associated with the crimes, but all that changed four years later, when, Michael Barrett (a former scrap-dealer from Liverpool, who subsequently claimed to have single-handedly brought about the IRA ceasefire as an agent of MI5) approached a literary agent, furtively using an assumed name and, presented them with a handwritten journal which he explained had been obtained from a friend shortly before he died. The diary describes in graphic detail, the deadly forays into London and clearly identifies the killer as James Maybrick,

The trial of Florence Maybrick.

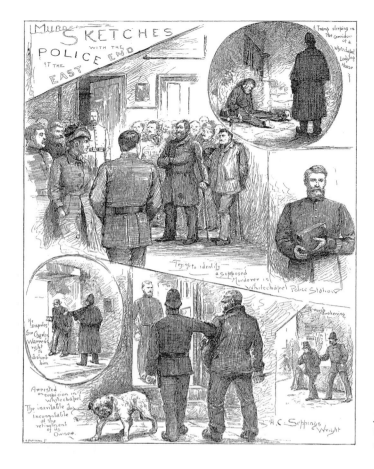

James Maybrick was never suspected during the police search for Jack the Ripper.

although the confessional document is signed 'Jack the Ripper' and dated 3 May 1889 – a week before the suspicious death of its alleged author. With Ripperologists reeling from the shock of this startling revelation, another Liverpudlian, Albert Johnson independently produced supporting evidence in the form of a gold watch made in 1846, which had scratched on the inner case the inscription 'J. Maybrick', the words 'I am Jack' and the initials of Mary Nichols, Annie Chapman, Elizabeth Stride, Catherine Eddowes and Mary Kelly. Little wonder that eyebrows were raised in disbelief with the realisation that James Maybrick had adopted a coat of arms with the cryptic motto *Tempus Omnia Revelat* – Time Reveals All.

Predictably, opinion was strongly divided about the authenticity of the document and the artefact. Before and after publication of the resulting best-selling crime book by Shirley Harrison, a swarm of Ripper buffs poured over the diary checking for errors of fact or language not in usage in the 1880s, while various scientific experts attempted to determine the age of the ink. The heated debate has produced contradictory results including the classic conclusion that the manuscript is 'either genuine, or a recent hoax'. Significantly, a graphologist found that the handwriting was not that of James Maybrick's and in 1994, Michael Barrett admitted in an interview with the *Liverpool Daily Post* that he had forged the diary. His solicitors rebutted the claim before the hoaxer responded by confessing all in a sworn affidavit.

21

James Kenneth Stephen
(1859-1892)

Flight of the Arrow

I suppose madness made him believe he was all powerful.

VIRGINIA WOOLF ON J.K. STEPHEN

Lawyer, journalist, poet and don, James Kenneth Stephen, belonged to the so-called intellectual aristocracy and professional elite. Known as 'J.K.' to his colleagues and 'Jem' to his friends, he and his illustrious family were blighted by insanity. Jem's cousin was the distinguished novelist Virginia Woolf, whose dark mood swings led to several failed suicide bids before she weighed down her pockets with stones and drowned herself, while, his father was the high court judge and writer Sir James Fitzjames Stephen, who spent his final days in an asylum after his failing mental faculties became all too noticeable during the murder trial of the unfortunate woman found guilty of poisoning her husband **James Maybrick**.

Two years before the death of his father, Jem Stephen also passed away in a mental institution. His increasingly odd behaviour had been precipitated by a blow to the head caused by an accident that occurred during a holiday in Felixstowe in 1886. Horse-riding along a bridal path on a cliff top, his mount was startled by the sound of a train whistle and threw him onto his head. Returning to London, he seemingly recovered following treatment from family physician **Sir William Gull** before his condition slowly deteriorated. Virginia Woolf recalled how, as a child, she had seen cousin Jem rush into her nursery, draw a blade from a swordstick and plunge it into a loaf of bread. In November 1891, Stephen was admitted to an asylum having been found in his room, stark naked and ranting, apparently suffering from the misapprehension that there was a warrant out for his arrest. According to a number of differing theories, this delusion may have been due to a guilty conscience brought about by his involvement in the East End Murders.

In 1883, Stephen was the tutor of the **Duke of Clarence** at Cambridge University, Michael Harrison in his book *Clarence* (1972) speculated that the two men were homosexual

77

Jem Stephen.

lovers and some of the poet's verse indicated misogyny – demonstrated in this extract from
A Thought:

> If all the harm that women have done
> Were put in a bottle and rolled into one,
> Earth would not hold it,
> The sky could not enfold it,
> It could not be lighted nor warmed by the sun,
> Such masses of evil would puzzle the devil
> And keep him in fuel while Time's wheels run.

Hatred and sadism was seemingly evident in his description of a 'loose-hipped, big-boned, disjointed,
angular' woman, perhaps a streetwalker described in the poem *In the Backs*: 'I did not like her: and I
should not mind, If she were done away with, killed or ploughed'. Harrison proposed that when the
affair with Clarence ended, Stephen went on a killing spree on dates significant to his former lover
such as royal birthdays and religious festivals. In this scenario, ten prostitutes were victims, acting out
the plot from one of his own poems, *Air Kaphoozelum*:

> For though he paid his women well,
> This syphilitic spawn of hell,
> Struck down each year and tolled the bell,
> For ten harlots of Jerusalem.

The theory was subsequently supported by a letter from Marny Hallam, published in the *Sunday
Times* in February 1975, who recounted that her great-grandfather, a barrister, had always expressed
the view that the authorities were aware that his contemporary J.K. Stephen was Jack the Ripper. The
poet has also been named as a co-murderer with Prince Albert Victor by forensic psychiatrist David

The victims formed an arrow pointing to Parliament.

Abrahamsen in *Murder and Madness* (1992) and, with Montague Druitt in John Wilding's *Jack the Ripper Revealed* (1993). In *The Ripper and the Royals* (1991), based on diaries produced by Joseph Gorman Sickert, purporting to have belonged to investigating police officer Inspector Abberline, Stephen is named as a member of the royal conspiracy covering up for the marital indiscretions of Prince Eddy, although the book's author, Melvyn Fairclough, later acknowledged that he no longer believes the diaries to be genuine. Alternatively, the research of Andy and Sue Parlour recorded in Kevin O'Donnell's *The Jack the Ripper Whitechapel Murders* (1997), discovered that a line drawn through the locations of the first four of the 'canonical' victims form an arrow pointing to the Houses of Parliament. The arrow is a Masonic symbol and purportedly the work of 'witty genius' Stephen who published two collections of poems *Lapsus Calami* (Flight of the Arrow) and *Quo Musa Tendis?* (Where the Muse Aims). With fellow lawyer Montague Druitt as a willing accomplice, the authors propose that Stephen was part of a conspiracy carried out on behalf of the **Prince of Wales**, who had impregnated the final Ripper victim Mary Kelly.

There is absolutely no tangible evidence to support the view that Jem Stephen had a sexual relationship with Prince Eddy or that he was even acquainted with Montague Druitt. All the speculation about any involvement in murder stems from the flawed motive of Michael Harrison who admitted in an interview with the *Listener* in 1972, that he had merely selected J.K. Stephen to develop the far-fetched suggestion of Dr Thomas Stowell that Prince Eddy was the Ripper. 'I didn't agree' he candidly revealed, 'but I couldn't leave the reader high and dry, so what I did was find somebody I thought was a likely candidate'.

22

Oscar Wilde
(1854-1900)

The Picture of Dorian Gray

One could never pay too high a price for any sensation.

OSCAR WILDE IN *THE PICTURE OF DORIAN GRAY*, 1891

In 1895, the glittering literary and social career of Oscar Wilde came to a ruinous conclusion through the scandalous revelations surrounding his close friendship with Lord Alfred 'Bosie' Douglas. His young companion's father, the Marquess of Queensbury, was determined to break up what he considered to be a 'loathsome and disgusting relationship' and deliberately set 'a booby trap' by delivering a card to the Irish wit signed 'To Oscar Wilde posing as a sodomite'. The insult had the desired effect when Wilde unwisely took the bait and had his tormentor arrested for criminal libel, leading to an ignominious fall from grace in the landmark 'Trials of Oscar Wilde'.

The author's legal action backfired disastrously when it became clear that the defendant had lined up a number of male prostitutes who were willing to give evidence of their sexual liaisons with Wilde. The case against Queensbury was hastily withdrawn and the accuser suddenly became the accused when he was arrested on charges of 'gross indecency' – a euphemism for any sexual encounter between males, which was then illegal. When the jury failed to reach a verdict, a re-trial was ordered

Oscar Wilde.

The Marquess of Queensbury.

and a crushed Wilde was resoundingly found 'guilty' and sentenced to two years hard labour where his torrid experience of prison life produced his last work of note, the epic poem *The Ballad of Reading Gaol*. Upon his release, the disgraced leader of the aesthetic movement exiled himself to France and, living frugally on the handouts of friends, passed away in a seedy hotel in 1900, famously remarking with typical Wildean wit, 'I am dying beyond my means'.

Author Ed Samms in *The Ghost of Oscar Wilde* (2000) makes the case that, as Wilde was part of the homosexual underground and also a Freemason, he knew of Prince Eddy's involvement in the Cleveland Street Scandal and the Masonic conspiracy to cover up the prince's secret marriage to a commoner in a spate of murders credited to Jack the Ripper. Echoes of both cases resonate in a macabre gothic novel written by Wilde in 1891. In a strange departure from his plays of upper-class manners and social intrigue, *The Picture of Dorian Gray* revolves around a painting of a young man whose prayers are answered to retain his youthful good looks while his portrait grows increasingly old. Having sold his soul, Gray leads a life of depravity in the East End of London, indulging in unspeakably loathsome practices until, tired of his evil life, he knifes to death the artist of his repulsive, decaying portrait, which, he then attempts to slash and destroy but inflicts a mortal wound on himself. Hearing a noise in the attic where the picture is secretly stored, Gray's servants find the picture, resplendent in its original form, alongside the 'withered, wrinkled' body of their master with a knife through his heart, who is only recognisable from the rings on his fingers.

Although the central character's secret vices are not explicit in the text, the homosexual overtones of the story are unmistakable and, with reference to the network of rent boys and aristocratic clients recently uncovered in the Cleveland Street scandal, The *Scots Observer* commented: 'If Mr Wilde can write for none but outlawed noblemen and perverted telegraph boys, the sooner he takes to tailoring (or some other decent trade) the better for his own reputation and the public morals'.

CLOSING SCENE AT THE OLD BAILEY.
TRIAL OF OSCAR WILDE

OSCAR WILDE AS A LECTURER 1882 AMERICA.

OSCAR WILDE AS A PRISONER 1895 BOW STREET.

JURY

SALE OF OSCAR WILDE'S EFFECTS

OSCAR WILDE'S HOUSE IN TITE STREET.

It is believed that the character of Dorian Gray was modelled on Jack the Ripper. In the story, Dorian is a member of a club in Whitechapel, a district where 'It was rumoured that he had been seen brawling with foreign sailors in a low den in the distant parts of Whitechapel, and that he had consorted with thieves and coiners and knew the mysteries of their trade'. The locality and the *modus operandi* of the Ripper are certainly reminiscent in the following passage: 'Where he went to he hardly knew. He remembered wandering through dimly lit streets, past gaunt black-shadowed archways and evil-looking houses. Women with hoarse voices and harsh laughter called after him. "So I have killed Sibyl Vane", said Dorian half to himself … '

In the biography *Oscar Wilde: A Gallic View of His Whole Extraordinary Career* (1968), author Philippe Julian noted, 'Oscar Wilde knew a duke whose eccentricities were so marked that he was suspected of being the untraced murderer Jack the Ripper'. This is an obvious reference to Prince Eddy, the Duke of Clarence, who could also be construed to be the thinly veiled object of Dorian Gray's comment, 'If Kent's silly son takes his wife from the streets, what is that to me?'

Much of the prosecution's case against Wilde centred on the perceived pornographic content of *The Picture of Dorian Gray*. In cross-examination, the author was questioned about how the hero of the book had ruined the lives of several other men 'including one who had committed suicide and another who had been obliged to leave England "with a tarnished name"'. The latter could easily refer to Lord Arthur Somerset who had gone abroad and escaped prosecution for his part in the Cleveland Street affair by threatening to implicate his friend Prince Eddy, while the former could refer to the death of another of the prince's acquaintances, Montague Druitt, who drowned himself in the River Thames in December 1888. Many years later, it was revealed that the police suspected the former lawyer and recently sacked teacher of being Jack the Ripper.

Ed Samms contends that by alluding to these cases in his novel, Wilde opened himself up to persecution when his own sexual secrets came out in court and it became 'imperative to put him away, lest the many answers to his many secrets would incriminate those with more to lose than some artist'. If, however, the 'artist' did have such incriminating information about Prince Eddy and his circle, surely he would have taken the option chosen by Lord Arthur Somerset and threatened to reveal all, unless the charges against him were dropped. It seems far more likely that the writer simply used a combination of inside information and real-life news stories to produce a cracking plot for his best-selling novel.

23

Frank Miles
(1852-1891)

FOR PITY AND LOVE

*It often seems to me that art conceals the artist far more completely
than it ever reveals him.*

OSCAR WILDE IN *THE PICTURE OF DORIAN GRAY* (1891)

Landscape gardener and artist Frank Miles exhibited the first of twenty-one works at the
Royal Academy in 1874, his success culminated with the award of the prestigious Turner Medal
for a landscape entitled *An Ocean Coast, Llangraviog, Cardiganshire,* in 1880. Overcoming the
considerable handicap of colour blindness, the favourable reception to his work justified the
confidence of fine-art tutor John Ruskin who had noted the young man's promise and airily
predicted 'With his love for his mother and his ability to paint clouds he must get on'.

While contemporary critics admired the flowing landscapes, Miles was to become best known
for incorporating his expert knowledge of flowers into his pastel sketches of society beauties,
including the mistresses of the **Prince of Wales**. Notable amongst these was Lillie Langtry,
who charmed a host of prominent men who were subsequently implicated in the hunt for Jack
the Ripper. Rising politician **Randolph Churchill** was spellbound by the way she conquered
London society wearing the only socially acceptable gown she owned – a simple black dress;
Liberal leader **William Gladstone** enjoyed sitting at her feet and reading poetry to her; while,
author **Oscar Wilde** displayed his adoration by sleeping on her doorstep and believed she was
'the loveliest woman in Europe'. The 'budding' actress agreed to have her first official portrait
drawn by Miles who appropriately depicted his subject against a background of lilies. Upon
completion, the work was acquired by another ardent admirer, Queen Victoria's son Prince
Leopold, who gave the likeness pride of place in his bedchamber at Buckingham Palace.

The 'Jersey Lily' sat for Miles at the home he shared with the 'professor of aesthetics'
– Oscar Wilde. The housemates had been introduced by a mutual friend, author and sculptor

Frank Miles.

Lord Ronald Gower, who had studied with Wilde at Oxford University before becoming a close friend and patron of Miles. Commissions for *Life* magazine attracted some of the great beauties of London to Miles' studio where they happily posed while being amused by the witty conversation and scintillating company of Wilde. Lillie Langtry even persuaded her royal beau the Prince of Wales to accompany her to meet Miles and Wilde and the heir to the throne humorously acknowledged that it was a privilege to be granted such an audience: 'I do not know Mr Wilde, and not to know Mr Wilde is not to be known'. Unfortunately, Oscar's growing fame and infamy led to an acrimonious split with Frank Miles. The two men were lampooned in a contemporary play about effeminate dandies called *The Grasshopper* and were the obvious inspiration for an operetta satirising aestheticism in Gilbert & Sullivan's *Patience*, and, when the eccentric author controversially published *Poems,* which was branded obscene by some critics, the whiff of scandal upset Miles' father, who threatened to cut off his son's allowance, unless

A sketch of Lillie Langtry by Frank Miles.

he immediately severed his association with Wilde. Reluctantly, Miles asked his friend to find alternative accommodation and the wounded poet's parting words for this act of betrayal were 'I will leave you. I will go now, and I will never speak to you again as long as I live'.

There has been unsubstantiated speculation that Frank Miles had male lovers including Oscar Wilde and the openly gay Lord Ronald Gower – the role model for the character of the decadent Lord Henry Wooton in Wilde's dark homoerotic novel *The Picture of Dorian Gray*. While the artist's probable relationships with fashionable homosexuals are cloaked in secrecy, his paedophilic tendencies became apparent when the police investigated his relationships with girls below the age of consent. Despite warnings about facing arrest for his sordid interest in young girls, he flouted convention by co-habiting with his under-age model, Sally Higgs, a former flower-seller, who was portrayed posing against a background of oriental flora in his acclaimed work *For Pity and Love* which was exhibited at the Royal Academy in 1882.

The artist had some intriguing links with the Whitechapel Murders. One of his relative's was an equerry to ill-fated heir presumptive, Prince Albert Victor, the **Duke of Clarence**, whose early death triggered royal conspiracy theories, whilst, Miles himself had served in the same

Miles was in an asylum during the reign of the 'East End Fiend'.

military regiment as the brother of leading police suspect Montague Druitt, who drowned himself in December 1888. A neighbour of Frank Miles was Sir Melville Macnaughten, appointed Assistant Commissioner of CID at Scotland Yard in 1889. Acknowledging that 'The truth will never be known, and did at one time lie at the bottom of the Thames', the police official reviewed the evidence and produced a memorandum concluding that the most likely culprit was Druitt, who, shortly before his death had been dismissed, for undisclosed reasons, from his teaching post at a private boys school. Macnaughten was convinced of Druitt's guilt adding, 'From private information I have little doubt but that his own family suspected this man of being the Whitechapel murderer; it was alleged that he was sexually insane'.

Frank Miles's tenuous relationship with suspicious characters and the nature of his sexuality stimulated correspondence from Thomas Toughill in the early 1970s, suggesting to pioneer Ripperologist Colin Wilson, that the artist himself might be responsible for the murderous assaults on East End prostitutes. Desite the fact that Miles suffered a complete breakdown of his mental health and was confined in an asylum at Brislington, near Bristol from 1887 until his death in 1891, Toughill pondered on his theory for half a lifetime before 'unveiling stunning evidence' in *The Ripper Code* (2008) demonstrating with 'devastating effect' that Jack the Ripper was indeed the 'former friend' of Oscar Wilde. Furthermore, utilising a 'coded message', the famed author 'dropped hints' about the murderous escapades in several of his works, notably *The Picture of Dorian Gray*.

24

Algernon Swinburne (1837-1909)

THE DEMONIAC POET

*A braggart in matters of vice, who had done everything he could
to convince his fellow citizens of his homosexuality and bestiality,
without being in the slightest degree a homosexual or bestialiser.*

OSCAR WILDE ON ALGERNON SWINBURNE

Classed alongside the literary genius of Byron and Shelley, Algernon Swinburne also shares with them the distinction of being among the few great poets to emerge from the English aristocracy. Described as a 'demoniac' child who skipped around the room reciting original poetry, Swinburne was the son of an admiral and the grandson of the Earl of Ashburnham. Educated at Eton, his psychological development was scarred when he discovered a perverse delight for the customary public school punishment of 'birching'. In adult life, he recalled the ecstasy of being beaten by figures of authority in numerous compositions including *The Flogging Block*, *The Schoolboy's Tragedy* and *A Boy's First Flogging*. The fledgling poet's masochistic tendencies were enhanced by his obsession with the works of the Marquis de Sade. They influenced and encouraged the inclusion of sexually charged stanzas that proliferated his first collection of *Poems and Ballads* published in 1866. Critically acclaimed with a mixture of outrage and admiration, the sheer brilliance of the decadent prose, without the use of obscene language or explicit descriptions of carnal pleasure, firmly established him as the leading poet of the day, while, the shocking themes of immorality and sensuality induced him to being humorously renamed 'Algernon Swineborn' by the satirical magazine *Punch*.

In his mid-twenties, Swinburne vowed never to marry after being bitterly disappointed in love. Having seemingly neglected to declare his romantic intentions to the object of his affections, he was devastated when his cousin Mary Gordon, entered into matrimony with a dashing army officer. The disconsolate poet bared his soul about his 'lost' love in *The Triumph of Time* and

Algernon Swinburne.

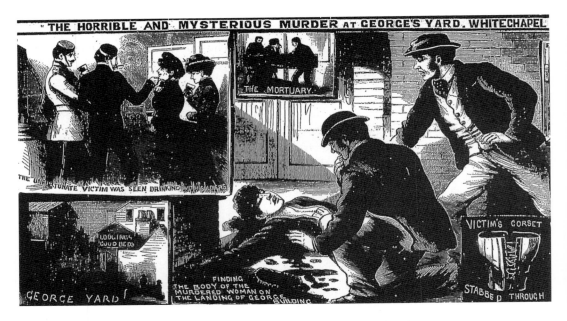

Swinburne did not consort with the 'down-market' whores of Whitechapel.

quoted a passage from it in a letter referring to the impending marriage of the recipient, literary critic Edmond Gosse:

> I suppose it must be the best thing that can befall a man to win and keep the woman that he loves while yet young; at any rate I can congratulate my friend on his good hap without any too jealous afterthought of the reverse experience which left my own young manhood 'a barren stock' — if I can cite that phrase without seeming to liken myself to a male Queen Elizabeth.

The lovelorn poet's sense of loss was furthered by the deaths of two other women he deeply cared for; his favourite sister Edith and Elizabeth Siddal, the wife of his friend, pre-Raphaelite artist Dante Gabriel Rosetti. The two men had met as students of Oxford University, where Swinburne was rusticated for his individualistic behaviour and failed to graduate, delighting in describing his academic career as ending 'in complete and scandalous failure'. Soon after leaving Oxford, he forged another important male friendship with explorer and adventurer Richard Burton, who had travelled the world recording the marriage customs of various peoples including the Mormons of Utah, where leader Brigham Young denied him permission to join the polygamous cult. Swinburne was recruited by Burton to join the Anthropology Society and its wilder offshoot the Cannibal Club whose culture of drunken debauchery was soon to have a detrimental effect on the poet. Cycles of excessive drinking followed by periods of drying out were to become a continuous feature of his life. As chronic alcoholism dimmed his poetic powers and he embarked upon a secondary career as a literary reviewer, rumours began to circulate that Swinburne was a homosexual. In 1867, while staying at the home of the recently widowed Rossetti, he supposedly disturbed the artist by sliding naked down the banisters with a boyfriend. His amenable host responded by encouraging his current escort Adah Isaacs Menken to introduce Swinburne to the joys of heterosexual lovemaking. The free-spirited actress had earned notoriety appearing dressed only in a pair of flesh coloured tights and tied to a horse riding bareback for her role in the sensational play *Mazeppa*. Wooed by countless men and married four times in the space of ten years, she initially had trouble coping with her new lover's pain threshold and complained, 'I can't make him understand that biting's no use'. Nevertheless, Swinburne's relationship with the American temptress endured until she journeyed to Paris where her outrageous lifestyle came to a premature end a few months later at the age of thirty-three. With her health deteriorating she wrote to a friend 'I am lost to art and life. Yet, when all is said and done, have I not at my age tasted more of life than most people who live to a hundred?'

To counter growing criticism of his sexual peccadilloes, Swinburne regaled listeners with wild tales of his perversions and particularly scandalised society by circulating a false story that he had engaged in pederasty and bestiality with a monkey – and then ate it. These sick outbursts caused **Oscar Wilde** to famously denounce his fellow writer as 'a braggart in matters of vice'. What is undeniably true is that Swinburne's mania for masochism was satisfied by constant visits to high-class flagellation brothels. Research by the acknowledged doyen of British crime writers Richard Whittington-Egan for *A Case Book on Jack the Ripper* (1975) led to the inclusion of Swinburne's name appearing in a list compiled from unlikely contemporary suspects who had been proposed as Jack the Ripper. As the poet's well documented sexual preference was for masochistic encounters with up-market courtesans in St John's Wood, it can only be what has been termed 'Algernonic exaggeration' about his sexual exploits that could possibly have lead anyone to have seriously accused him of sadistic attacks on down-market whores in the East End.

25

Dr Thomas Barnado
(1845-1905)

THE SCIENTIFIC HUMANITARIAN

Men like Dr Barnado have the faults of their qualities and the
vices of their virtues.

WILLIAM T. STEAD

On 19 September 1888, the editor of the *Pall Mall Gazette*, William T. Stead, proposed the theory that the Whitechapel Murders had been carried out by a 'scientific humanitarian' in order to highlight the suffering of the poor in the East End where, confirmed by a correspondent of *The Times*, 'tens of thousands of our fellow creatures are begotten and reared in an atmosphere of godless brutality, a species of human sewage, the very drainage of the vilest productions of ordinary vice'. Stead argued that by overcoming the theological argument about the taking of life, the 'maximum effect' had been achieved by 'a minimum expenditure of money and life'. Murder was commonplace, therefore, a 'scientific sociologist' had selected 'drunken, vicious, miserable wretches, whom it was almost a charity to relieve of the penalty of existence', then horribly mutilated his victims to attract sensational publicity, which, in turn, benefited the wider community where 'the class which of all others suffers the most hideous and tragic fate in the human lot'.

The journalist was certainly correct in asserting that Jack the Ripper had succeeded where the prayers of the Church and the charity of philanthropists had failed in awakening the public conscience to the existence of, what an inquiry into the 'condition of the abject poor', conducted by the Revd Andrew Mearns in 1883, had termed 'The Bitter Cry of Outcast London'. One man who had dedicated his life to the poor of the East End was Dr Thomas Barnado. In 1866, he left his home in Dublin and journeyed to London, initially hoping to be accepted for missionary work in China, before enrolling as a medical student at the London Hospital in Whitechapel, then opening a Ragged School for the children of the poor in Stepney. One of his pupils, Jim

Dr Barnado with Jim Jarvis.

Jarvis, made him aware of the vast numbers of homeless children sleeping rough and stirred the doctor into action to help relieve their suffering and deprivation with the provision of shelters and was subsequently credited with rescuing 60,000 children from the streets in his lifetime.

With little patronage or influence, he toiled for twenty years, before the heart of the nation was stirred by publicity given to the ghastly crimes, then 'stimulated by the recently revealed Whitechapel horrors' he outlined his vision in a letter to the editor of *The Times* as a 'voice raised on behalf of the children' which was published 9 October 1888. In it, he also revealed that he had gone to the mortuary and identified the body of Elizabeth Stride – having met her with a group of prostitutes at the house where she lodged only four nights before her death:

> The company soon recognized me, and the conversation turned upon the previous murders. The female inmates of the kitchen seemed thoroughly frightened at the dangers to which they were presumably exposed. In an explanatory fashion I put before them the scheme which had suggested itself to my mind, by which children at all events could be saved from the contamination of the common lodging-houses and the streets, and so to some extent the supply cut off which feeds the vast ocean of misery in this great city.

Jim Jarvis reveals London's abandoned 'street Arabs'.

The pathetic part of my story is that my remarks were manifestly followed with deep interest by all the women. Not a single scoffing voice was raised in ridicule or opposition. One poor creature, who had evidently been drinking, exclaimed somewhat bitterly to the following effect: 'We're all up to no good, and no one cares what becomes of us. Perhaps some of us will be killed next!' And then she added, 'If anybody had helped the likes of us long ago we would never have come to this!'

'Murder as Advertisement' – the title of William T. Stead's article – might easily apply to the work of Barnado, whose familiarity with the locality and its inhabitants has led his name to be suggested as a suspect for the killings, firstly by Donald Rumbelow in *Identity of Jack the Ripper* (1959) and by Gary Rowlands in an essay *The Mad Doctor* (1999). Barnado was a stressed individual who suffered several nervous breakdowns during his career and the case against him emanates from psychological scarring caused by his lonely childhood and problematic youth which was overtaken by religious zeal and a desire to impose his will and clear prostitutes from the streets as their trade was producing unwanted pregnancies and creating the desperate situation of London's abandoned 'street Arabs'. This 'down on whores' attitude coupled with his anatomical knowledge provided the motive and means to take calculated drastic action and resolve the issue. Having also worked as a journalist in London, Barnado had an insight into

Feeding the hungry in a 'Ragged School' in London.

A common
lodging house
in Flower and
Dean Street
where Elizabeth
Stride lived.

how to manipulate the press by keeping the story to the forefront of the news by submitting the letters to the press that were signed 'Jack the Ripper'. Rowlands argues that the killings only stopped when the doctor became profoundly deaf following an accident in a swimming pool that rendered him incapable of listening out for sounds, such as the approaching footsteps of a patrolling policeman when he was enacting a crime.

Barnado was embroiled in scandal when two of his fiercest critics, Baptist minister, the Revd George Reynolds and temperance philanthropist Frederick Charrington accused the happily married doctor of frequently 'walking arm in arm with prostitutes' and persuaded his former landlady, forced into the world's oldest profession following the death of her spouse, to allege that she had earlier engaged in an adulterous relationship with Barnado during his days as a medical student, while her husband was away at sea. It is significant, however, that although Barnado's religious beliefs as a member of the Plymouth Brethren prevented him from suing his detractors, the matter was heard before a court of arbitration which totally exonerated him of all the fabricated smears against his character. Likewise, Dr Barnado's cause had merely benefited inadvertently by the activities of an anonymous serial killer and in another editorial about the spate of violent deaths, William T. Stead commented:

> The question to-day, however, is not how to kill but how to stay alive. And the public, for a moment conscience-stricken at the spectacle of how the poor live, will gladly co-operate with Dr. Barnardo if he can utilize his vast experience so as to help in establishing a self-supporting decent dossing ken for the homeless children of London.

26

Francis Thompson
(1859-1907)

In Darkest London

Whether man's heart or life it be which yields
Thee harvest, must Thy harvest fields
Be dunged with rotten death.

FROM *THE HOUND OF HEAVEN*
FRANCIS THOMPSON (1888)

Lancastrian poet and writer Francis Joseph Thompson came from a respectable Roman Catholic family. Influenced by his parent's fervent religious beliefs, Francis was educated with a view to joining the Church and his sister recalled that her brother 'wished to be a priest from a little boy'. However, his suspect temperament and love of romantic literature led his teachers to deem him unsuitable for the priesthood and he decided to followed in his father's footsteps and become a physician. Undergoing training in Manchester, the student struggled for six years and failed his final medical examinations three times. At the age of twenty-one, he witnessed the lingering death of his mother whose painful suffering from liver disease could only be relieved by administering opium – a drug which quickly became an addiction for her bereaved son when he was prescribed laudanum for a lung infection.

When it became patently obvious he would not succeed in the medical profession, Thompson broke away from his family and moved to London in 1885, hoping to become a writer. Scratching a meagre living by selling matches or calling cabs, any money he earned was squandered on opium that influenced the stark imagery of his poetry. However, his inability to impress publishers with his work caused him to sink into a deep depression. By autumn 1887, abject failure had forced him to live on the streets and the vagrant was contemplating suicide when the turning point in his life occurred. Wandering homeless around the dockland area of London, he met a prostitute who took him into her lodgings and cared for him throughout that

A scramble for soup tickets by the homeless in London.

winter. The name of the streetwalker or the exact nature of her relationship with Thompson was not recorded in his notes, but it is clear that she encouraged him to continue writing verse and at Easter 1888, the Catholic literary journal *Merry England* published one of his religious poems *The Passion of Mary*. The editor Wilfred Meynell had been trying to trace the whereabouts of the author who had submitted the work a year earlier signing it 'Yours with little hope' and forlornly requesting 'Kindly address your rejection to the Charing Cross Post Office'.

Recognising Thompson's brilliance, Meynell and his wife offered Thompson a home, but the poet was reluctant to leave the woman who had rescued him until she suddenly disappeared from the lodgings – fully aware that her presence would deny him a golden opportunity to further his career. Gone from his life forever, Thompson showed his gratitude for her kindness in many of his subsequent poems.

Temporarily overcoming his drug addiction after a period of withdrawal in a monastery, Thompson emerged invigorated to produce two major poems *Ode to the Setting Sun* and his

Dr Barnado's serving dinner to 1,200 of London's aged poor in 1888.

best-known work *The Hound of Heaven* which examines the theme of death and rebirth with the fleeing human soul being remorselessly pursued by God.

With his newfound fame, Thompson attacked the prevailing social conditions of the poor, notably in the essay *In Darkest London* published in 1891. Drawing on his own experiences to highlight the inadequacy of provision for the homeless and destitute, he criticised legislation that made an unforgiving distinction between 'deserving' and 'undeserving' poor. Despite the outstanding work of **Dr Barnado** and the Salvation Army, founded by **General William Booth**, shelters and soup kitchens provided scant relief to an unrelenting life of misery and poverty.

Ultimately, the author's dependence on drugs reduced his weight to only five stone and drove him to an early grave. Apart from a trunk full of unpublished jottings, his only legacy was a toy theatre he had coveted since his childhood and a few opium pipes which had been the instruments of his sad demise. Living in London with his protectors and patrons the Meynell family at the time of the Whitechapel Murders, the poet was not suspected until recently when his name was proposed on the Casebook: Jack the Ripper website by Richard Patterson. Highlighting the fact that all of the murders were all committed on the feast days of the Roman Catholic saints, Patterson views Thompson on a mission from God, disposing of sinners and avoiding capture by seeking sanctuary in Christ Church, Whitechapel. Apart from his abandoned preparation for the priesthood, Thompson also attracts suspicion through his medical training, his habit of carrying a surgical scalpel and the ownership of a leather apron. Such a garment became the focus of the police investigation following the death of the first 'canonical' victim 'Polly' Nichols. Prostitutes in the area told the police that a sinister individual demanding money with menaces from them had accosted them. The culprit wore a leather apron, carried a sharp knife and frequently threatened, 'I'll rip you up'. Described as short, thickset and moustachioed, it was reported that the man dubbed 'Leather Apron' had been seen in other parts of London hanging around common lodging houses – drawing parallels with the search conducted by Thompson after he had been deserted by the 'tart with a heart'. However, all the witnesses described the suspect as a foreigner with a strong Semitic appearance, which discounts Thompson. Following the discovery of a leather apron close to the body of Annie Chapman, there was a frenzy of anti-Semitic activity and angry mobs took to the streets beating up anyone of Jewish appearance asserting that 'No Englishman would commit such murders'.

During his medical training, Francis Thompson displayed a nightmarish horror of the operating theatre and dissecting room, therefore, it is unthinkable that, even under the influence of drugs, he could have savagely killed and removed the organs of women. The 'Leather Apron' scare came to an end when John Pizer, a 'crazy Jew' from Poland, was arrested and identified as the man responsible for habitually harassing prostitutes although, he was conclusively cleared of being Jack the Ripper.

27

General William Booth
(1829-1912)

ONWARD CHRISTIAN SOLDIERS

The first vital step in saving outcasts consists in making them feel
that some decent human being cares enough for them to take an
interest in the question whether they are to rise or sink.

THE DOCTRINE OF WILLIAM BOOTH CITED BY WILLIAM
JAMES IN *THE VARIETIES OF RELIGIOUS EXPERIENCE* (1985)

The elusiveness of Jack the Ripper has led some people to believe that the killer was a person who could pass easily through the streets without raising suspicion, perhaps blending in with the surroundings dressed in the respectable uniform of a soldier, policeman or a member of the Salvation Army. In 1865, fire and brimstone preacher, William Booth, had founded the East London Revival Society in Whitechapel. Ironically, in view of his temperance views, the movement's headquarters were originally based at an ex-public house the Eastern Star. The religious organisation's 'volunteer army' rapidly spread to other cities and was reorganised on military lines and renamed the Salvation Army in 1878, with 'General' Booth leading his 'Christian soldiers' into the battle for people's souls. Booth also underwent a 'conversion' when, distressed at the plight of the urban poor, he inexorably became a social reformer. Quickly establishing himself as the champion of the deprived, social shelters were provided to provide the basic daily needs of displaced persons. As he once explained, he had nothing against utopianism, collectivist or individualism, but 'here in our Shelters last night were a thousand hungry, workless people … It is in the meantime that the people must be fed, that their life's work must be done or left undone forever'.

Faced with the social problem of the link between poverty and vice, the Salvation Army also undertook rescue work among prostitutes who were shunned by other religious bodies. Newspaper editor **William T. Stead** was persuaded to undertake a crusade highlighting the

General William Booth.

trade of child prostitution in a shocking series *The Maiden Tribute of Modern Babylon* published in the *Pall Mall Gazette* in 1885. The journalist was also the ghostwriter who crystallised William Booth's thought-provoking proposals for the relief of unemployment and homelessness in a classic literary work on poverty *In Darkest England and the Way Out* (1890).

William Booth genuinely believed that eternal punishment was the fate of all those who died without conversion – obituaries published in the Salvation Army journal *War Cry* never referred to 'death' – they triumphantly announced that a 'brother' or 'sister' had 'gone to Glory' or been 'suddenly promoted' to enter the Pearly Gates of Heaven. Therefore, perhaps, an overzealous foot soldier decided to take matters into his or her own hands and alleviate the misery and suffering in Whitechapel by 'promoting' street walkers from the lowest class of human depravity to the highest state of the hereafter and ultimate salvation. Crime historian Colin Wilson – a pioneer of modern research into the East End Murders and the man who first coined the phrase 'Ripperologist' – heard gruesome tales about the 'East End Fiend' from his maternal grandfather, who could remember being warned in his childhood to get indoors by 6 p.m. or run the risk of

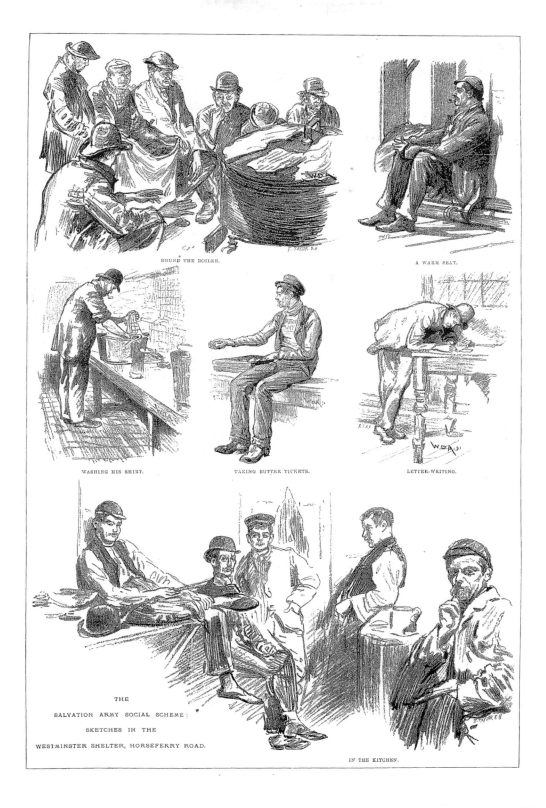

ROUND THE BOILER.

A WARM SEAT.

WASHING HIS SHIRT.

TAKING BUTTER TICKETS.

LETTER-WRITING.

THE
SALVATION ARMY SOCIAL SCHEME:
SKETCHES IN THE
WESTMINSTER SHELTER, HORSEFERRY ROAD.

IN THE KITCHEN.

being accosted by Jack the Ripper. In September 1939, the young Wilson read an article about the case in the weekly magazine *Titbits* that, as a grown-up author he recalled in a series 'My Search for Jack the Ripper' published by the *Evening Standard* in 1960. Mistakenly claiming that General William Booth of the Salvation Army, had expressed his belief that the Whitechapel Murders were committed by his own secretary, a man who had 'dreams of blood' and, once told him that 'Carrotty Nell will be the next to go'. Of course, Booth could not have made this startling revelation at the outset of the Second World War as he had been 'promoted to Glory' over a quarter of a century earlier, but trusting faithfully in his memory, Wilson published his faulty recollection without rechecking the source of his story. This factual error remained in circulation for over forty years, until a Scotland Yard librarian discovered that, in actuality, the *Titbits* article quoted had been the memoir of a Salvation Army Commissioner, David Lamb, who was convinced that the killer was a signwriter he had employed. The unnamed man had 'visions of blood' and made the chilling prophecy about Carrotty Nell shortly before she was murdered in February 1891. Frances Coles was the real name of Carroty Nell, who is one of several women largely discounted by Ripperologists as being a victim of Jack the Ripper.

The death of Frances Coles alias Carrotty Nell.

A policeman discovered her body in a passageway beneath some railway arches. She had just been assaulted and the blood still flowed from the cut in her throat. The victim briefly opened her eyes then passed away as the officer blew his whistle to summon assistance. A post-mortem examination by two doctors concluded that the fatal wound had been inflicted after her assailant had flung her to the ground. The prostitute's clothes had not been interfered with and there were none of the telltale slashes to the abdomen, consistent with the *modus operandi* of Jack the Ripper.

Whether or not, Frances Coles alias Carrotty Nell, was the final victim of the Ripper, Colin Wilson, long respected as a 'clearing house for theories' developed by up-and-coming Ripperologists, rightly contends that her killer could not have been the signwriter cited by Commissioner Lamb, for it seems highly unlikely that a murderer would risk apprehension by announcing his target in advance to a God-fearing, law-abiding, high-ranking officer of the Salvation Army. Unfortunately, despite a lifelong fight to eradicate the demons of crime and prostitution in the poverty-ridden battleground of Whitechapel, General William Booth is not known to have expressed any theory of his own that would shed light on the investigation to identity Jack the Ripper.

28

George Gissing
(1857-1903)

THE NETHER WORLD

Gissing's novels are a protest against the form of self-torture that
goes by the name of respectability.

H.G. WELLS IN *GEORGE GISSING* 1948

Socio-realist novelist George Gissing's works were often critically dismissed in contemporary reviews as 'gloomy' or 'despondent' for their bleak depiction of the lower stratum of society marked by graphic observations of squalor and human misery in Victorian London. The pessimistic view of the world reflected in his books was coloured by bitter personal experience. His own youthful middle-class aspirations had been crushed by a self-inflicted downfall, rendering him, in his own words, one of 'a class of young men distinctive of our time – well educated, fairly bred, but without money'.

A brilliant scholar, Gissing's troubles began while he was a star pupil at Owens College, Manchester, where he was awarded glittering prizes and secured a promise of entry to London University. In 1876, any dreams and ambitions of an academic career in the classics were destroyed by scandal when he became infatuated with Nell Harrison, a young prostitute whom he attempted to reform by lending financial support. Foolishly, he raised the money by resorting to crime, stealing cash from his fellow students. Acting on repeated reports of theft, the college authorities assigned a detective to the cloakrooms where the horrified culprit was caught red-handed. Expulsion and imprisonment were the consequences of his misguided actions. Feeling acutely ashamed after serving one month's hard labour at Bellevue Prison, the disgraced Gissing fled to America for a year earning a meagre living writing articles for a Chicago newspaper. Penniless and friendless, he returned to England and, settling in London, compounded his earlier error of judgement by entering into a doomed marriage with Nell. Utilising his education to produce an income by private tutoring, Gissing used a small legacy to self-publish his first

George Gissing.

novel, *Workers in the Dawn*, a semi-autobiographical story about an idealistic man and his sluttish wife – a raw study of the most desperate levels of poverty-stricken life in London. Although it paved the way for future literary acclaim, pricking the social conscience in the same way as the late Charles Dickens, the gritty book was a complete commercial failure, selling fewer than fifty copies during the first six months of publication. His marriage also failed as his wife fought a losing battle with the bottle and frequently lapsed into prostitution causing the gradual disintegration of the relationship. The couple separated and, at the age of only twenty-nine, Nell succumbed to the ravages of alcohol abuse and venereal disease. At the beginning of March 1888, her husband recalled movingly in his diary of being summoned to a lodging house in Lambeth to identify the body. The small room with its pitiful scattering of personal effects and sticks of furniture was described in heartbreaking detail. Despite paying his wife a generous weekly allowance, Gissing noted a number of pawn tickets which, he realised, had been redeemed for the purpose of obtaining drink, overcoming her desire to abstain, proved by the presence of three cards which she had signed in a forlorn attempt to 'take the pledge'. The only food was 'a little

Unemployed people in the East End apply for poor relief.

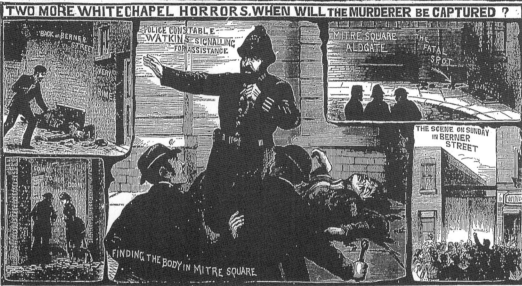

Gissing read about the 'double event' deaths of Liz Stride and Katie Eddowes in Paris.

bit of butter and a crust of bread' found in a drawer – 'the most pitiful sight my eyes ever looked upon'. The author then gazed at his wife for the last time: 'She lay on the bed covered with a sheet. I looked long, long at her face, but could not recognize it. It is more than three years, I think, since I saw her, and she had changed horribly.' Since committing theft for the object of his affections, Gissing's conscience had been tortured by the 'guilty secret' of his crime and this latest turn of events left him reeling with shock:

> Came home to a bad, wretched night. In nothing am I to blame; I did my utmost; again and again I had her back to me. Fate was too strong. But as I stood beside that bed, I felt that my life henceforth had a firmer purpose. Henceforth I never cease to bear testimony against the accursed social order that brings about things of this kind. I feel that she will help me more in her death than she balked me during her life. Poor, poor thing!

These intense feelings of despair were transformed into a superb evocation of tragic squalor, in the greatest of George Gissing's 'slum novels' *The Nether World* completed in July 1888 and published in April 1889. Punctuated with humour and pathos in its portrayal of the poor, the story's artistic merit was recognised by the reviewer of *Public Opinion*: 'Those who can appreciate a realism quite on the Dickens plan, but without the perpetual farce that takes one's attention off the hideousness of London poverty, will find plenty of it in these three volumes, which cannot fail to add much to his growing reputation'.

The timing of the stark contents of this book, the author's abhorrence of working-class life and his anguish over the tragic death of his estranged spouse have naturally led to conjecture that he wreaked vengeance for his miserable existence on the whores of Whitechapel. While an author's wit can be likened to a rapier and the pen is said to be mightier than the sword, a critic of the *Daily News* once darkly compared Gissing's writing to another lethal weapon: 'The knife with which he probes the wound is sometimes roughly handled, but it is held by one who well knows what he is doing'. In *A Case Book on Jack the Ripper* (1975), respected crime historian Richard Whittington-Egan Thompson revealed that Gissing was contemporarily muted as the serial killer. However, the author had a watertight alibi, for, upon completing *Nether World*, he sold the copyright to his publisher, giving him the means to indulge a long-held wish to tour France and Italy where he spent a prolonged period from autumn 1888 to Spring 1889. Gissing's diary confirms that when the 'double event' killings of Elizabeth Stride and Katherine Eddowes occurred on 30 September, he was located in Paris where two days later he sought news about the lurid adventures of his nemesis Jack the Ripper, 'Walked about the Palais Royal, thence to Madeleine to buy the *Standard*, in order to read of the two new murders in Whitechapel … '

29

Lewis Carrol
(1832-1898)

THE MAD HATTER

I wonder if I've been changed in the night? Let me think. Was I the same when I got up this morning? I almost think I can remember feeling a little different. But if I'm not the same, the next question is 'Who in the world am I?' Ah, that's the great puzzle!

QUOTATION FROM *ALICE'S ADVENTURES IN WONDERLAND* (1865)

As Jack the Ripper stalked the East End, an illustration of a ghoul, floating like a spectre over the poverty-stricken, crime-ridden slums, was published with an accompanying verse by the satirical magazine *Punch*, 29 September 1888:

> Look at these walls; they reek with dirt and damp,
> But in the shadows crouched, the homeless tramp
> May huddle undisturbed the black night through.
> These narrow winding courts – in thought – pursue.
> No light there breaks upon the bludgeoned wife,
> No flash of day arrests the lifted knife,
> There shrieks arouse not, nor do groans afright.
> These are but normal noises of the night …
> … Must it be
> That the black slum shall furnish sanctuary
> To all light shunning creatures of the slime,
> Vermin of vice, carnivora of crime?

The artist of this famous work entitled *The Nemesis of Neglect* was Sir John Tenniel, renowned illustrator of the classic children's story *Alice's Adventures in Wonderland* and its sequel *Through the Looking Glass* written by Lewis Carroll – the pseudonym of the Revd Charles Dodgson. The cleric's love of anagrams led Richard Wallace to deduce in *Jack the Ripper, Light Hearted Friend* (1996), that Carroll had revealed important clues in his work alluding to the fact that he was the perpetrator of the Whitechapel Murders. An example of the illuminating evidence appears in this extract from *Jabberwocky*:

> 'Twas brillig, and the slithy toves
> Did gyre and gimble in the wabe:
> All mimsy were the borogoves,
> And the mome raths outgrabe.

Upon further analysis, the anagram in the nonsense verse is untangled and translates into a chilling confession:

> Bet I beat my glands til,
> With hand-sword I slay the evil gender.
> A slimey theme; borrow gloves,
> And masturbate the hog more!

Educated at Rugby, the public school immortalised by the novel *Tom Brown's Schooldays*, Lewis Carroll recalled terrible memories of the bullying regime and homosexual encounters: 'I cannot say ... that any earthly considerations would induce me to go through my three years again ... I can honestly say that if I could have been ... secure from annoyance at night, the hardships of the daily life would have been comparative trifles to bear'.

Rejecting a career in the Church in favour of accepting a mathematics fellowship at Christ Church, Oxford University, Carroll remained unmarried. He had no romantic attachments to mature women and openly admitted 'I am fond of children (except boys)'. His inspiration for sending 'my heroine down a rabbit hole' was 'to please a child I loved' – the Dean of Christ Church's daughter, Alice Liddell. The author dedicated all his books to little girls of his acquaintance and many of his biographers have concluded that he had an unhealthy interest in under-age females whom he habitually escorted un-chaperoned. Gossip about his unconventional relationships vexed him and caused him to give up his hobby of photographing young women clad in revealing bathing suits. Although Carroll has been portrayed as a paedophile, there is no clear evidence to suggest his interest was sexually motivated. Paradoxically, his obsession with the company of ingénues clears him of any involvement in the deaths of the prostitutes, for, when four of the victims were killed, the author was on summer vacation at his holiday home in Eastbourne accompanied by his guest, Isa Bowman – a fourteen-year-old child actress chosen to play the role of Alice in a stage production. In addition, when excerpts from Wallace's book appeared in *Harper's Magazine*, the first paragraph read:

> This is my story of Jack the Ripper, the man behind Britain's worst unsolved murders. It is a story that points to the unlikeliest of suspects: a man who wrote children's stories. That man

THE NEMESIS OF NEGLECT.

"THERE FLOATS A PHANTOM ON THE SLUM'S FOUL AIR,
    SHAPING, TO EYES WHICH HAVE THE GIFT OF SEEING,
INTO THE SPECTRE OF THAT LOATHLY LAIR,
    FACE IT—FOR VAIN IS FLEEING!
RED-HANDED, RUTHLESS, FURTIVE, UNERECT,
'TIS MURDEROUS CRIME—THE NEMESIS OF NEGLECT!"

Lewis Carrol.

is Charles Dodgson, better known as Lewis Carrol, author of such beloved books as *Alice in Wonderland*.

Two readers demonstrated the absurdity of this theory by producing their own anagram by brilliantly rearranging the passage into a murder confession:

The truth is: I, Richard Wallace, stabbed and killed a muted Nicole Brown in cold blood, severing the throat with my trusty shiv's strokes. I set up Orenthal James Simpson, who is utterly innocent of this murder. P.S. I also wrote Shakespeare's sonnets, and a lot of Francis Bacon's works too.

30

William Gladstone
(1809-1898)

THE GRAND OLD MAN

He has been the very madman of politics from the point of view
of Mr. Worldly-Wiseman.

W. T. STEAD, *REVIEW OF REVIEWS*, APRIL 1892

Jack the Ripper is often portrayed as a toff, attired in evening dress, cloak and top hat, carrying his paraphernalia of death in a Gladstone bag – a portmanteau named after a politician who himself has been suspected of perpetrating the Whitechapel Murders.

William Ewart Gladstone served as Prime Minister in four governments and in the opinion of commentator **William T. Stead**, there was one significant blot on a sixty-year political career in the House of Commons – his appalling record on women's rights:

Probably no man in Parliament has had more cause than he to recognise the inspiration, the sustaining strength, and the consolation of female friendship. He has been brought into close personal relations with some of the best and with some of the most unfortunate of the sex. From the Queen upon the throne to the Magdalen in the street for whose redemption he has laboured, all have ministered to him in one way and another, and yet, at the close of a long life, no statesman has seemed so stolid and so persistently blind to the injustices under which women labour.

Queen Victoria did not disguise her hatred of Gladstone famously remarking 'He speaks to me, as if I was a public meeting' and his arrogant belief in the inferiority of women was reinforced as he obstinately opposed the use of birth control, the introduction of divorce laws, moves to prevent the traffic in under-age vice and the repeal of legislation which imprisoned prostitutes if they refused to undergo medical tests for sexually transmitted diseases. Social reformer

THE GRAND OLD MAGICIAN'S IRISH POLICY.

An 1886 Beecham's advert for Gladstone's 'wonderful remedy' for the 'Irish problem'.

William Gladstone.

Josephine Butler criticised the attitude of men such as Gladstone when she commented 'Men … hypocritically cloaked their own sensuality in the outward garb of punishing the being whom they alone brought to shame'. Secretly, Gladstone recorded in his diaries that he was troubled by thoughts of women as a source of purely sexual pleasure, which, was at odds with his religious upbringing and his marriage vows. A fascination with prostitutes began when he became involved in the Engagement, a secretive lay religious group for whom he embarked on 'rescue' work with fallen women, inviting them to his home for tea and improving conversation where he found himself having to resist sexual temptation. Tormented by pornographic thoughts, he began to flagellate himself as a spiritual and physical punishment after encounters with harlots he was supposed to be aiding, admitting to himself that he 'courted evil'.

Physical relations with his wife Catherine seemingly ceased after she had conceived nine times in fifteen years. Thereafter, her husband's sexual frustration was relieved by tree-felling on his estate – which, to commentators of the day seemed an unusual spare-time pursuit for one of the world's most powerful men. William T. Stead observed the total concentration needed for the activity in a sly innuendo: 'In chopping down a tree you have not time to think of anything excepting where your next stroke will fall', and Charles Dodgson alias **Lewis Carroll** conjured up an amusing anagram of William Ewart Gladstone converting the name to 'A wild man will go at trees'.

Gladstone was busy felling trees after the Liberal Party's General Election victory in 1868, when he received a telegram from the Queen asking him to form his first government and he immediately vowed, 'My mission is to pacify Ireland'. His determination to find an answer to the 'Irish question' inevitably resulted in failure. Refusing to be deflected by the Phoenix Park Murders during his second term of office in 1882, he made a pact with jailed Irish Nationalist Party leader **Charles Parnell** using his ally's lover Katherine O'Shea to act as go-between. Fighting and losing an election campaign in 1886 on the single issue of Home Rule for Ireland, then surviving the fallout from scandal of the subsequent divorce of Katharine O'Shea, with Parnell named as co-respondent in 1890, Gladstone finally passed a bill for Home Rule which, was defeated in the House of Lords, bringing down the curtain on the octogenarian's long career in 1893.

Following his resignation, Gladstone drew up a new will and made a sworn declaration attesting his marital fidelity. He did this to protect his family from rumours circulating about his interest in fallen women and his strange involvement with lay preacher and ex-courtesan Laura Thistlethwayte. Since 1864, Gladstone had enjoyed what has been described as 'a platonic extra-marital affair' with the woman he addressed as his 'Dear Spirit'. She, unlike the prostitutes he attempted to redeem, had already been saved from a life of sin and married to a man of substance who subsequently died from a self-inflicted bullet wound in 1887. Totally obsessed by the object of his affection, Gladstone kept in constant touch with a stream of potentially damaging correspondence and personal visits to her home. When the Thistlethwaytes found themselves pursued by creditors in 1878, court proceedings revealed embarrassing details of the besotted female's expenditure on lavish gifts for Gladstone, one of them being a ring that he continued to wear on the third finger of his right hand. In 1894, the bizarre relationship was ended by her death and only hospitalisation for an unsuccessful cataract operation prevented the ailing former Prime Minister from attending her funeral.

Perverse contradictory thoughts of sexual gratification while supposedly fighting the social evil of prostitution have given rise to unconvincing and totally unfounded suggestions that at the age of seventy-eight, the half-blind politician, conducted a violent crusade to put an end to vice in Whitechapel. This is not the first occasion that he was branded a killer, for, in 1885, the Premier's controversial handling of the crisis in the Sudan, where national hero General Gordon lost his life in the fall of Khartoum, provoked an angry response from his Tory opponents. The acronym applied by his Liberals supporter, GOM (Grand Old Man) was pointedly reversed to MOG (Murderer of Gordon).

31

W.G. Grace
(1848-1915)

THE COMIC BANDIT

Of course, you don't have to be a public figure to be suspected of being Jack the Ripper, but it does seem to help.

MARK WHITEHEAD AND MIRIAM RIVETT
IN *JACK THE RIPPER* (2001)

Crime writer Monsignor Ronald Knox once wryly suggested that **William Gladstone** and W.G. Grace were one and the same person leading a double-life. His jocular comment referred to the fact that the two men were equally prominent as the two most famous Englishmen of their day. Strange, therefore, that while the 'Grand Old Man' of politics has been credited with suspicion that it was his hand which committed the Whitechapel Murders, the 'Old Man' of cricket has been passed over for this dubious accolade. Surely, the time has come for this oversight to be remedied, for, Dr William Gilbert Grace, recognisable to everyone simply by his initials 'W.G.', has impeccable credentials, as a medical man and eminent personality, to fit the ideal profile of Jack the Ripper.

England's greatest cricketer was born in Bristol, one of five brothers who all followed their father's profession and trained to become doctors at the medical school attached to Bristol Royal Infirmary. W.G.'s tutor was Robert Tibbets a surgeon who gloried in the nickname 'Slasher'. An image of W.G. is conjured up in an early history of the medical establishment which describes one burly, bearded student whose imposing presence 'represented a terrible aspect in the operation room, with saws, forceps, and knives stuck into his belt, looking very much like a comic bandit'. W.G. took eleven years from 1868-1879 to complete his medical training; his progress as a 'perpetual student' was understandably impeded by his achievements on the cricket field for Gloucestershire and England. Dominating the game for almost half a century, he set batting and bowling records that elevated him to legendary status. W.G.'s reputation occasionally

Gladstone – the face of the Ripper?

suffered through scandal in the family. In 1883, Dr Edward Mills Grace, known as 'The Coroner' – a professional position he fulfilled in Bristol – was hauled before the courts to answer charges of dereliction of duty when he chose to hold inquests on only half of the thirty-two cases of sudden death referred to him by the police. Significantly, these lapses 'occurred chiefly in the months of July and August' when 'E.M.' was otherwise engaged appearing on the cricket field alongside his illustrious brother W.G. After listening to a catalogue of explanations and excuses from the defendant, the magistrates dismissed the case on condition that 'Dr Grace would in future adhere more closely to the directions of the Lord Chancellor as to the duties of Coroners'. W.G. also tried to hush up an embarrassing matter when another cricketing relative fell from 'grace'. His cousin, Walter Raleigh Gilbert, experienced financial problems in 1886 and, in addition to playing for Gloucestershire, tried to raise extra funds appearing as the club professional for Cheltenham. Foolishly, he also supplemented his income by stealing money from the dressing room. The thief was caught rifling through his team-mates pockets and sentenced to twenty-eight-days hard labour. Upon his release from prison, the family packed him off to Canada where he remained for the rest of his days. The cricket 'bible' Wisden drew a veil over the career of Gilbert 'about whose disappearance from cricket there is no need to speak'.

Could the 'bandit' trained by 'Slasher' have been the 'Ripper'? On 18 July 1888, W.G. celebrated his fortieth birthday, although any midlife crisis was seemingly averted by his appointment to captain the national side for the first time. Already one down in the series of three matches against Australia, the England side immediately squared the series under their new skipper then, triumphantly won the 'Ashes' with victory at Old Trafford on 31 August − several hours after the body of the first canonical 'Ripper' victim Mary Ann Nichols was discovered in London. Likewise, the next target, Annie Chapman, was found early in the morning of 8 September, the day that W.G. finished on the winning side for Lord Londesborough's XI against

A Case of Mistaken Identity? This contemporary cartoon reveals that 'W.G.' bore an uncanny resemblance to another prime minister implicated in the Ripper case − Lord Salisbury.

Australia at the Scarborough Festival. W.G.'s presence at cricket grounds so far away from the scene of the crimes would seem to eliminate him from the investigation, however, his frequent mercenary travels to well-paid cricket engagements around the country, earning him a fortune and making a mockery of his 'amateur' status, has led biographers to note that he was far more conversant with railway timetables than medical books. Apart from providing him with a perfect alibi, an overnight return rail journey would not have tired him, nor impaired his performance on the field of play. On one renowned occasion, he stayed up all night to deliver a baby, and then took the field to score a double century for his county. The celebrated man behind the beard had disgusting personal habits, rarely washed, was often guilty of blatant gamesmanship and displayed a boorish schoolboy humour verging on callousness. After attending the birth of a stillborn child, he allegedly commented, 'The baby's dead, the mother's in a bad way, but I think I can save the father'. If the argument against Grace seems unconvincing, consider the case of Montague Druitt who was also playing cricket outside London on the day of one of the murders, yet, has remained a leading suspect since he was sacked under a cloud from his job as a schoolmaster and drowned himself in the River Thames in December 1888.

Of course, W.G. Grace, shares one thing in common with every other celebrity named in this book, he was not Jack the Ripper – although, the Bishop of Hereford obviously sensed some latent potential for evil when he made a curious comment in an after dinner speech to commemorate the cricketing legend's 100th century in 1895, observing that, had the guest of honour been born in Ancient Greece 'he would have had the pleasure of killing a great number of people and of being sung in immortal verse'. No doubt 'W.G.' was content to be lauded for his sporting 'battles'. In the famous cricket poem *At Lords*, maligned 'Ripper' suspect **Francis Thompson** recalled a fiercely fought contest between his native Lancashire and Gloucestershire:

> A Shire so young that has scarce impressed its traces,
> Ah, how shall it stand before all-resistless Graces?
> O, little red rose, their bats are as maces
> To beat thee down, this summer long ago!

Bibliography and Sources

General Sources

Anon, *Illustrated History of the Nineteenth Century*, Rochester, Grange Books 2000

Begg, Paul, Fido Martin, Skimmer Keith, *The Jack the Ripper A-Z*, London, Headline Book Publishing Plc 1991

Curtis, L. Perry, *Jack the Ripper and the London Press*, New Haven, London, Yale University Press 2001

Davenport-Hines, Richard, *Jack the Ripper* in *Oxford Dictionary of National Biography*, Matthew, H.C.G., Harris, Brian, (eds) Oxford, Oxford University Press 2004

Morgan, Giles, *Freemasonry*, Harpenden, Pocket Essentials 2007

Morley, Christopher J., *Jack the Ripper: A Suspect Guide*. E-book 2005

Website: Casebook: Jack the Ripper (www.casebook.org)

Queen Victoria: A Reign of Terror

Fairclough, Melvyn, *The Ripper and the Royals,* London, Duckworth 1991

Knight, Stephen, *Jack the Ripper: The Final Solution* London, Harrap 1976

Matthew, H.C.G., Reynolds, K.D., *Queen Victoria* in *Oxford Dictionary of National Biography*, Matthew, H.C.G., Harris, Brian (eds) Oxford, Oxford University Press 2004

The Prince of Wales: The Playboy Prince

Matthew, H.C.G., *Edward VII* in *Oxford Dictionary of National Biography*, Matthew, H.C.G., Harris, Brian (eds) Oxford, Oxford University Press 2004

O'Donnell, Kevin, *The Jack the Ripper Whitechapel Murders*, St Osyth, Ten Bells Publishing 1997

Wilding, John, *Jack the Ripper Revealed*, London, Constable 1993

Joseph Merrick: The Elephant Man

Osborne, Peter, *Joseph Carey Merrick* in *Oxford Dictionary of National Biography*, Matthew, H.C.G., Harris, Brian (eds) Oxford, Oxford University Press 2004

Treves, Frederick, *The Elephant Man and Other Reminiscences*, London, Cassel & Co. 1923

Journals and magazines: *The Times*

Joseph Carey, Merrick Tribute Website @ www.jsitton.pwp.blueyonder.co.uk

Richard Mansfield: The Strange Case of Dr Jekyll and Mr Hyde

Wilstach, Paul, *Richard Mansfied: The Man and the Actor*, New York, Scribner's 1908

Journals and magazines: *Daily News, Daily Telegraph, New York Times, London Times*

Charles Parnell: The Uncrowned King of Ireland

Bew, Paul, *Charles Stewart Parnell* in *Oxford Dictionary of National Biography*, Matthew, H.C.G., Harris, Brian, (eds) Oxford, Oxford University Press 2004

Journals and magazines: *Illustrated London News, Judy, Pall Mall Gazette, New York Post, The Times*

Lord Salisbury: An Honest Politician

Knight, Stephen, *Jack the Ripper: The Final Solution,* London, Harrap 1976

Smith, Paul, *Robert Arthur Talbot Gascoyne-Cecil, The Third Marquess of Salisbury* in *Oxford Dictionary of National Biography*, Matthew, H.C.G., Harris, Brian (eds) Oxford, Oxford University Press 2004

Warren, Nick, 'The Great Conspiracy' in *The Mammoth Book of Jack the Ripper*, Eds Jakubowski, Maxim and Braund, Nathan, London, Robinson Publishing 1999

Journals and magazines: *The Times*

Lord Randolph Churchill: The Fourth Party

Fairclough, Melvyn, *The Ripper and the Royals,* London, Duckworth 1991

Leslie, Anita, *Jennie: The Life of Lady Randolph Churchill*, London, Hutchinson 1969

Quinault, Roland, *Lord Randolph Henry Spencer Churchill* in *Oxford Dictionary of National Biography*, Matthew, H.C.G., Harris, Brian, (eds) Oxford, Oxford University Press 2004

Sir Charles Warren: Hounded Out of Office

Knight, Stephen, *Jack the Ripper: The Final Solution,* London, Harrap 1976

Surridge, Keith, *Sir Charles Warren* in *Oxford Dictionary of National Biography*, Matthew, H.C.G., Harris, Brian, (eds) Oxford, Oxford University Press 2004

Journals and magazines: *Judy, Star, Times*

The Duke of Clarence: The Prince of Darkness

Fairclough, Melvyn, *The Ripper and the Royals*, London, Duckworth 1991

Knight, Stephen, *Jack the Ripper: The Final Solution*, London, Harrap 1976

Stowell, Dr Thomas, 'Jack the Ripper – A Solution?' *Criminologist*, November 1970

Van der Kiste, John, *Prince Albert Victor,* in *Oxford Dictionary of National Biography*, Matthew, H.C.G., Harris, Brian, (eds) Oxford, Oxford University Press 2004

Sir William Gull: Physician Extraordinary

Hervey, Nick, *Sir William Withey Gull* in *Oxford Dictionary of National Biography*, Matthew, H.C.G., and Harris, Brian, (eds) Oxford, Oxford University Press 2004

Knight, Stephen, *Jack the Ripper: The Final Solution*, London, Harrap 1976

Spiering, Frank, Prince *Jack: The True Story of Jack the Ripper*, USA Doubleday 1978

Stowell, Thomas, 'Jack the Ripper - A Solution?' *Criminologist*, November 1970

Journals and magazines: *Le Gaulois, The Times*

Sir Robert Anderson: The Third Man

Anderson, Robert, *The Lighter Side of My Official Life*, London, Hodder & Stoughton 1910

Knight, Stephen, *Jack the Ripper: The Final Solution,* London, Harrap 1976

Porter, Bernard, *Sir Robert Anderson* in *Oxford Dictionary of National Biography*, Matthew, H.C.G., Harris, Brian, (eds) Oxford, Oxford University Press 2004

Walter Sickert: Jack the Ripper's Bedroom

Baron, Wendy, *Walter Richard Sickert* in *Oxford Dictionary of National Biography*, Matthew, H.C.G., Harris, Brian, (eds) Oxford, Oxford University Press 2004

Cornwell, Patricia, *Portrait of a Killer: Jack the Ripper – Case Closed*, London, Little, Brown 2002

Melvyn Fairclough, *The Ripper and the Royals* London, Duckworth 1991

Fuller, Jean Overton, Sickert *and the Ripper Crimes*, Oxford, Mandrake 1990

Knight, Stephen, Jack *the Ripper: The Final Solution*, London, Harrap 1976

Sturgis, Matthew, *Walter Sickert: A Life*, London, Harper Perennial 2005

King Leopold II: The Barbaric Beast of the Belgian Congo

Farson, Daniel, *Jack the Ripper*, London, Michael Joseph 1972

Journals and magazines: *The Review of Reviews*

Website: Heroes & Killers of the 20th century @ moreorless.au.com

Robert James Lees: The Human Bloodhound

Journals and magazines: *Ilfracombe Chronicle*, *Leicester Mercury*, *Chicago Sunday Times-Herald*

Website: Robert James Lees @ www.rjlees.co.uk

William T. Stead: Shock Journalism

Baylen, Joseph O., William Thomas Stead, in *Oxford Dictionary of National Biography*, Matthew, H.C.G., Harris, Brian, (eds) Oxford, Oxford University Press 2004

Harris, Melvyn, *Jack the Ripper: The Bloody Truth*, London, Columbus 1987

Journals and magazines: *East Anglican Daily Times*, *Pall Mall Gazette*, *Review of Reviews*

Website: Robert James Lees@www.rjlees.co.uk

William T. Stead and the *Pall Mall Gazette* @ www.attackingthedevil.co.uk

Aleister Crowley: The Wickedest Man in the World

Anon, Aleister Crowley and Jack the Ripper, Cambridge, published privately 1988

Decker, Ronald, *Aleister Crowley* in *Oxford Dictionary of National Biography*, Matthew, H.C.G., Harris, Brian, (eds) Oxford, Oxford University Press 2004

Whitechapel, Simon, 'Guts 'n' Roses' in *The Mammoth Book of Jack the Ripper*, Jakubowski, Maxim, Braund, Nathan (eds). London, Robinson Publishing 1999

Symonds, John, Grant, Kenneth, (eds) *The Confessions of Aleister Crowley*, London, Routledge & Keegan Paul 1979

Journals and magazines: *Empire News*, *Pall Mall Gazette*

Madame Helena Blavatsky: Jill the Ripper

Anon, *Aleister Crowley and Jack the Ripper*, Cambridge, published privately 1988

Davenport-Hines, Richard, *Helena Petrovna Blavatsky* in *Oxford Dictionary of National Biography*, Matthew, H.C.G., Harris, Brian (eds) Oxford, Oxford University Press 2004

Journals and magazines: *Illustrated London News*, *Pall Mall Gazette*, *Review of Reviews*, *The Times*

Sir Arthur Conan Doyle: The Adventures of Sherlock Holmes

Edwards, Owen Dudley, Sir Arthur Ignatius Conan Doyle in *Oxford Dictionary of National Biography*, Matthew, H.C.G., Harris, Brian (eds) Oxford, Oxford University Press 2004

Garrick-Steele, Rodger, *The House of the Baskervilles*, USA Authorhouse 2003

Hardeen, George, *The Secret Life of Houdini,* 2007

Spiering, Frank, *Prince Jack: The True Story of Jack the Ripper*, USA Doubleday 1978

Wagner, E.J., *The Science of Sherlock Holmes, from Baskerville Hall to the Valley of Fear, the real forensics behind the great detective's cases*, Hoboken, New Jersey 2006

Rasputin: Great Criminals of Russia

Le Quex, William, *Things I Know About Kings, Celebrities and Crooks*, London, E. Nash & Grayson 1923

McCormick, Donald, *The Identity of Jack the Ripper*, London, Jarrolds 1959

James Maybrick: The Diary of Jack the Ripper

Davenport-Hines, Richard, *Florence Elizabeth Maybrick* in *Oxford Dictionary of National Biography*, Matthew, H.C.G., Harris, Brian, (eds) Oxford, Oxford University Press 2004

Harrison, Shirley, *The Diary of Jack the Ripper*, London, Smith-Gryphon 1993

Harrison, Shirley, 'The Diary of Jack the Ripper' in *The Mammoth Book of Jack the Ripper*, London, Robinson Publishing 1999

Journals and magazines: *Liverpool Daily Post*

James Kenneth Stephen: Flight of the Arrow

Abrahamsen, David, *Murder and Madness: The Secret Life of Jack the Ripper*, USA, Dutton Books 1992

Fairclough, Melvyn, *The Ripper and the Royals*, London, Duckworth 1991

Harrison, Michael, *Clarence: the Life of HRH the Duke of Clarence and Avondale 1864-1892*, London, W.H. Allen 1972

O'Donnell, Kevin, *The Jack the Ripper Whitechapel Murders*, St Osyth, Ten Bells Publishing 1997

Smith, K.J.M., *Sir James Fitzjames Stephen* in *Oxford Dictionary of National Biography*, Matthew, H.C.G., Harris, Brian, (eds) Oxford, Oxford University Press 2004

Wilding, John, *Jack the Ripper Revealed*, London, Constable 1993

Journals and magazines: *The Times, The Sunday Times*

Oscar Wilde: The Picture of Dorian Gray

Calloway, Stephen, Colvin, David, *The Exquisite Life of Oscar Wilde*, London, Orion Media 1997

Edwards, Owen Dudley, *Oscar Fingal O'Flahertie Wills Wilde* in *Oxford Dictionary of National Biography*, Matthew, H.C.G., Harris, Brian, (eds) Oxford, Oxford University Press 2004

Julian, Philippe, *Oscar Wilde: A Gallic View of His Whole Extraordinary Career, Drawing on Fresh Sources*, New York, Viking Press 1968

Sams, Ed, *The Ghost of Oscar Wilde*, USA, Yellow Tulip Press 2000

Journals and magazines: *The Scots Observer*

Frank Miles: For Pity and Love

Calloway, Stephen, Colvin, David, *The Exquisite Life of Oscar Wilde*, London, Orion Media 1997

Beatty, Laura, *Lillie Langtry: Manners, Masks and Morals*, London, Chatto & Windus 1999

Potter, Matthew C., *George Francis Miles* in *Oxford Dictionary of National Biography*, Matthew, H.C.G., Harris, Brian, (eds) Oxford, Oxford University Press 2004

Toughill, Thomas, *The Ripper Code*, Stroud, The History Press 2008

Algernon Swinburne: The Demoniac Poet

Rooksby, Rikky, *Algernon Charles Swinburne* in *Oxford Dictionary of National Biography*, Matthew, H.C.G., Harris, Brian, (eds) Oxford, Oxford University Press 2004

Whittington-Egan, Richard, *A Case Book on Jack the Ripper*, London, Wildy & Sons 1975

Dr Thomas Barnado: The Scientific Humanitarian

McCormick, Donald, *Identity of Jack the Ripper* (revised ed) London, Long 1970

Rowlands, Gary, *The Mad Doctor* in *The Mammoth Book of Jack the Ripper*, Maxim Jakubowski and Nathan Braund (eds) London, Robinson Publishing 1999

Wagner, Gillian, *Barnado*, London, Weidenfeld and Nicolson 1979

Williams, A.E., *Barnado of Stepney*, London, George Allen & Unwin 1923

Journals and magazines: *Pall Mall Gazette, Times*

Francis Thompson: In Darkest London

Boardman, Brigid M., *Francis Joseph Thompson* in *Oxford Dictionary of National Biography*, Matthew, H.C.G., Harris, Brian, (eds) Oxford, Oxford University Press 2004

Patterson, Richard, *Francis Thompson*, Casebook: Jack the Ripper @ www.casebook.org

General William Booth: Onward Christian Soldiers

Booth, William, *In Darkest England and the Way Out* London, International Headquarters 1890

Wilson, Colin, 'A Lifetime in Ripperology' in *The Mammoth Book of Jack the Ripper*, Jakubowski, Maxim and Braund, Nathan (eds), London, Robinson Publishing 1999

Prochaska, Frank, *William Booth* in *Oxford Dictionary of National Biography*, Matthew, H.C.G., Harris, Brian (eds) Oxford, Oxford University Press 2004

Journals and Magazines: *Evening News, Times, Tit Bits, Pall Mall Gazette, War Cry*

George Gissing: The Nether World

Coustillass, Pierre (ed). *London and the Life of Literature in Late Victorian England: The Diary of George Gissing, Novelist*, Hassocks, Sussex, The Harvester Press 1978

Coustillass, Pierre, Partidge, Colin (eds). *Gissing: The Critical Heritage*, London and Boston. Routledge & Regan Paul 1972

Whittington-Egan Thompson, Richard, *A Case Book on Jack the Ripper*, London, Wildy and Sons 1975

Journals and magazines: *Daily News, Public Opinion*

Lewis Carrol: The Mad Hatter

Cohen Morton N., *Charles Lutwidge Dodgson* in *Oxford Dictionary of National Biography*, Matthew, HCG, Harris, Brian (eds) Oxford, Oxford University Press 2004

Furniss, Harry, *Some Victorian Men*, London, John Lane The Bodley Head Ltd 1924

Wallace, Richard, *Jack the Ripper, Light Hearted Friend*, USA, Gemini Press 1996

Journals and magazines: *Harper's Magazine*

Website: Looking for Lewis Carroll @ www.lewiscarrol.cc

William Gladstone: The Grand Old Man

Matthew, H.C.G., *William Ewart Gladstone* in *Oxford Dictionary of National Biography*, Matthew, H.C.G., Harris, Brian (eds) Oxford, Oxford University Press 2004

Website: William T Stead and the Pall Mall Gazette @

Journals and magazines: *Review of Reviews*

W.G. Grace: The Comic Bandit

Howat, Gerald MD, *William Gilbert Grace* in *Oxford Dictionary of National Biography*, Matthew, H.C.G., Harris, Brian (eds) Oxford, Oxford University Press 2004

Low, Robert, *W.G. Grace: An Intimate Biography*, London, Metro Publishing 2004

Munro Smith, G.A. *History of the Bristol Royal Infirmary*, Bristol 1917

Journals and magazines: *The Times*

Murder & Crime: Devon

MIKE HOLGATE

With its beautiful coastline and mild climate, Devon is well known as a tourist destination, but its many historic towns and windswept cliffs have darker and more sinister stories to tell. These tales from Devon's past reveal the county's connections with world-famous crime and murder cases. With more than sixty illustrations, this chilling book is bound to captivate anyone interested in Devon's dark history.

978 0 7524 4504 5

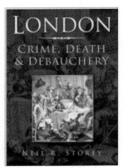

London Crime, Death and Debauchery

NEIL R. STOREY

London: Crime, Death & Debauchery is an alternative history of the darker side of Britain's capital city. No other book on London covers this topic in such a complete fashion, with cases ranging from the Restoration to the early nineteenth century. It weaves macabre accounts into an entertaining criminal history accessible to all.

978 0 7509 4624 7

Hanged at Pentonville

STEVE FIELDING

Over the years the high walls of London's Pentonville Prison have contained some of the most infamous criminals. Taking over from the dreaded Newgate Gaol at the turn of the century as the place of execution for north London and surrounding counties, over a hundred murderers and spies paid the ultimate penalty here. Steve Fielding has fully researched all these cases, and they are collected together here in one volume for the first time.

978 0 7509 4950 7

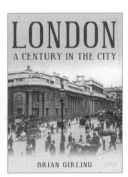

CENTURY IN THE CITY

BRIAN GIRLING

Utilising rare and unseen photographs including haunting images form the mid-nineteenth century, the book offers an exploration and celebration of A the City of London through a century from the 1850s to the 1960s. We may mourn the passing of that which was familiar to us, but perhaps this book will revive a half-forgotten memory or reveal times we never knew in a city which is known and loved worldwide.

978 07524 4507 6

If you are interested in purchasing other books published by The History Press, or in case you have difficulty finding any History Press books in your local bookshop, you can also place orders directly through our website

www.thehistorypress.co.uk